Santa Clara County Free Library

REFERENCE

$12.50

Mountain Wild Flowers
of the Pacific Northwest

This book spans the gap between technical floras on wild flowers of the Pacific Northwest, and short, or abridged treatments. The flowers here were selected — then photographed — because of their frequency of occurrence and ecological importance, as well as their attractiveness. The text has been designed for the general reader, but for students and teachers there are concise technical descriptions of each species, as well as a detailed botanical key. A glossary, complete index and interesting notes on the edibility of various plants are also included. The carefully selected natural-color photographs illustrating each species will simplify identification, and be a source of enjoyment in their own right.

Besides its usefulness as a field guide, *Mountain Wild Flowers of the Pacific Northwest* will be a welcome addition to the libraries of outdoor enthusiasts and all who appreciate the beauty of the wild.

Mountain Wild Flowers

of the Pacific Northwest

By Ronald J. Taylor
and
George W. Douglas

Photographs
by
Lee Mann and Ronald J. Taylor

Binford & Mort

Thomas Binford, Publisher

2536 S.E. Eleventh • Portland, Oregon 97202

The authors would like to acknowledge the valuable assistance of Gloria Taylor, in the preparation of this book, and of Patricia Claus and Joy Dabney, who did the illustrations. The cover photograph, by Lee Mann, shows wild flowers in the Mount Rainier area.

Library of Congress Cataloging in Publication Data

Taylor, Ronald J   1932-
    Mountain wild flowers of the Pacific Northwest.

    Includes indexes.
    1. Alpine flora—Northwest, Pacific—Identification.
    2. Wild flowers—Northwest, Pacific—Identification.
    I. Douglas, George W., 1938 (June 22)—joint author.
    II. Title.
QK144.T36   582'.13'09795   73-89237
ISBN 0-8323-0230-9
ISBN 0-8323-0231-7 pbk.

*Mountain Wild Flowers
of the Pacific Northwest*

Printed in the United States of America

First Edition

CONTENTS

INTRODUCTION

In an era of environmental awareness, people are trying more and more to identify with the outdoors. They are seeing new beauty there and deriving enjoyment and self-satisfaction from learning more about the diversity and intricacies of nature. *Mountain Wild Flowers of the Pacific Northwest* is a field guide for such persons. It is unique in that it combines color photography and non-technical descriptions with a systematic treatment complete with an identification key. It has been designed to span the gap between non-systematic popular treatments and existing technical floras. It should serve equally well from high school through college, where it will be useful in "local flora" classes. Also, the language is sufficiently non-technical for the book to be used by the outdoor buff or anyone who would ask the question, "What plant is that?"

The wild flowers included in this book were selected because of their ecological importance, the attractiveness of their flowers, or some unusual feature making them conspicuous in the field. However, some of the most widespread and important flowering plants, such as grasses and sedges, have not been included because of their lack of showiness and, especially, the difficulty of distinguishing the various species without technical training.

Identification

From the beginning of time, man has been a classifier; he has been concerned with the application of names to all manner of things. A name is an aid to communication, a means by which something can be discussed without elaborate description. Furthermore, there must be consistency in the usage of a name; therefore, in this book the Latin name of the species has been included immediately after the common name. In many cases the common name given here is only one of several, the one considered most appropriate and/or most widely recognized.

Common to all field guides is the problem of the scientific language which is often necessary for accurate distinction among organisms. The present authors have devoted considerable effort to avoid technical terminology not essential for identification. Still, the reader must be able to recognize flower parts and leaf structure, the characters by which flowering plants are most readily distinguished.

6

As an aid to this, labeled floral diagrams and illustrations of leaf structure have been provided, together with a glossary of terms. Also, a key for identification is included. Keys greatly facilitate identification of unknown organisms even though their attempted use often leads to frustration and eventual disregard by some untrained individuals. The key in this book has been kept simple and hopefully functional. Yet is must be acknowledged that there is some wisdom in the cliché that a key works well only for the one who wrote it.

Vegetative Zones

Although the mountainous regions of the Pacific Northwest are extremely variable geologically, environmentally, and therefore floristically, for purposes of convenience the entire area can be divided into three very general vegetative zones: the Continuous Forest Zone, the Mountain Meadow or Subalpine Zone, and the Alpine Zone. It is difficult, however, to clearly distinguish between the latter two zones and the distribution of many species spans both. Therefore, to make this book more functional, the plants have been arranged alphabetically, by common name, into two groups, those that "prefer" the shady, moist habitats of the continuous forest and those that occur on open, sunny slopes or in meadows of the Alpine and Subalpine Zones.

Continuous Forest Zone

The mature or climax forests of the Pacific Northwest are dominated by species of hemlock (*Tsuga*) and/or true fir (*Abies*). Frequent associates or occasional dominants include one—or a combination of—Douglas Fir, Pacific Red Cedar, Alaskan Yellow Cedar, and deciduous species such as maple, birch, and alder. Although the type and combination of tree species have varying effects on environmental factors—such as light intensity and soil chemistry, moisture, and structure—the Continuous Forest Zone is far more uniform than the other zones. There is, of course, a direct correlation between the degree of environmental variation and number of representative species. Therefore, in the continuous forests, with the restrictive light intensity and environmental uniformity, there are relatively few flowering plants. These plants—like mosses and ferns—are widely

7

and more or less regularly distributed, shade tolerant, and strongly competitive.

Widespread flowering plants of the forest include Foam Flower (*Tiarella*), Ground Dogwood (*Cornus canadensis*), Queen's Cup (*Clintonia uniflora*), Pipsissewa (*Chimaphila*), Wintergreen (*Pyrola*), Strawberry Bramble (*Rubus pedatus*), Twin Flower (*Linnaea borealis*), Fool's Huckleberry (*Menziesia ferruginea*), and Huckleberry (*Vaccinium*). Along streams or seepage areas, Devil's Club (*Oplopanax horridum*) and species of *Ribes* (Wild Currant) are common. In drier sites—and often associated with Douglas Fir—are Salal (*Gaultheria shallon*) and Oregon Grape (*Berberis nervosa*). Along the forest edge and in openings, many large shrubby species occur, such as Thimbleberry (*Rubus parviflora*), Salmonberry (*Rubus spectabilis*), and Red Elderberry (*Sambucus racemosa*).

Mountain Meadow Zone

Unlike the Continuous Forest Zone, the Mountain Meadow Zone is highly discontinuous. Meadow areas occur in avalanche tracks and other moist montane habitats which are unsuitable for forest growth, usually as a result of late snow melt. With sufficient soil, the vegetation of these sites is lush and variable, including both shrubs and herbs. Trees often appear to be invading mountain meadows and tree clumps may become established. In and around these clumps a mixture of meadow and forest species grows.

Common meadow shrubs include Thimbleberry, Salmonberry, Mountain Ash (*Sorbus*), willow (*Salix*), Mountain Alder (*Alnus sinuata*), and others. Some of the more conspicuous herbaceous representatives are Glacier Lily (*Erythronium grandiflorum*), Valerian (*Valeriana sitchensis*), Mountain Bistort (*Polygonum bistortoides*), Spring Beauty (*Claytonia lanceolata*), Columbine (*Aquilegia formosa*), Lousewort (*Pedicularis bracteosa*), Tiger Lily (*Lilium columbianum*), Fairy Bell (*Disporum hookeri*), Tall Yellow Violet (*Viola glabella*), False Hellebore (*Veratrum viride*), and many grasses and sedges. Along streams and seepage areas, Pink Monkey Flower (*Mimulus lewisii*), Bog Orchids (*Habenaria*), and various species of saxifrages (*Saxifraga*) are conspicuous. The heathers (*Phyllodoce* and *Cassiope*) are common representatives of the Alpine and Subalpine Zones.

Alpine Zone

The Alpine Zone is the region above the timberline, including the krummholz belt or area of stunted tree growth. This zone is characterized by extreme temperatures, high winds, dry summers, and thin, rocky soils often subjected to frost heaving and other important factors of erosion. Alpine plants are necessarily hardy and well adapted to the rigorous environment. Most of them have low cushion-like forms which protect them from wind damage and desiccation. Also, most alpine plants are conspicuously hairy—another protective adaptation, particularly against water loss.

Flowers of alpine species are usually large and showy, or in colorful clusters. Their attractiveness increases the efficiency of pollination by the numerous insects of the high mountains.

The Alpine Zone, because of its environmental diversity, has many different communities and an equally variable flora. Its most frequent plants include the heathers, daisies (*Erigeron*), saxifrages, stonecrops (*Sedum*), various members of the mustard and pink families (*Cruciferae* and *Caryophyllaceae* respectively), potentillas (*Potentilla*), paintbrushes (*Castilleja*), Partridge Foot (*Luetkea*), penstemons (*Penstemon*), Mountain Avens (*Dryas*), and many species of grasses and sedges.

Flowering Time

The sequence of flowering among representative species is consistent from year to year and changes little from one geographical area to another. The actual time of flowering, however, varies considerably because of yearly climatic fluctuations and factors such as slope effect, drainage patterns, and altitude. Because of these variants there has been no attempt to cite flowering time on a month-by-month basis; rather, it has been related to the seasons, bearing in mind that seasonal progression is dependent upon the factors cited above.

FLORAL STRUCTURES AND PARTS
REGULAR FLOWERS (RADIAL SYMMETRY)

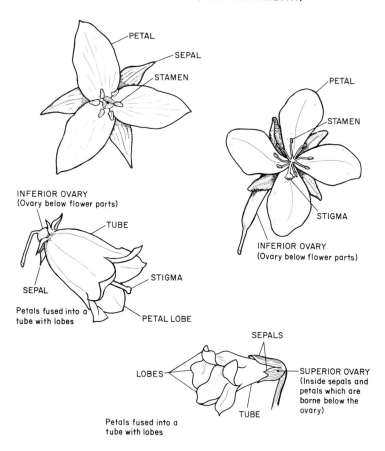

PETAL

SEPAL

STAMEN

PETAL

STAMEN

STIGMA

INFERIOR OVARY
(Ovary below flower parts)

INFERIOR OVARY
(Ovary below flower parts)

TUBE

STIGMA

SEPAL

Petals fused into a
tube with lobes

PETAL LOBE

SEPALS

LOBES

SUPERIOR OVARY
(Inside sepals and
petals which are
borne below the
ovary)

TUBE

Petals fused into a
tube with lobes

IRREGULAR FLOWERS (BILATERAL SYMMETRY)

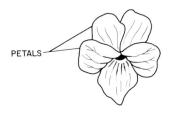

PETALS

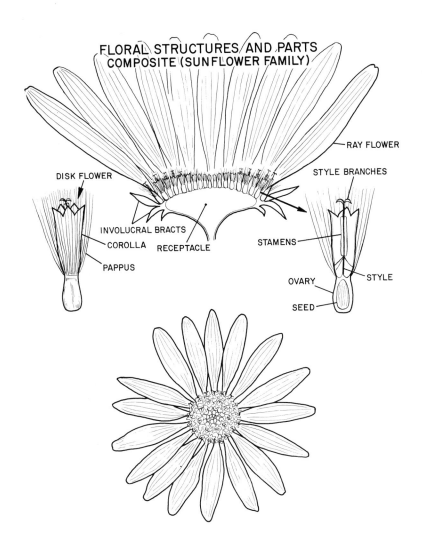

FLORAL STRUCTURES AND PARTS
COMPOSITE (SUNFLOWER FAMILY)

RAY FLOWER

DISK FLOWER

STYLE BRANCHES

INVOLUCRAL BRACTS

COROLLA   RECEPTACLE

STAMENS

PAPPUS

OVARY

STYLE

SEED

LEAF TYPE AND SHAPE

COMPOUND LEAVES (LEAVES DIVIDED TO THE MIDVEIN)

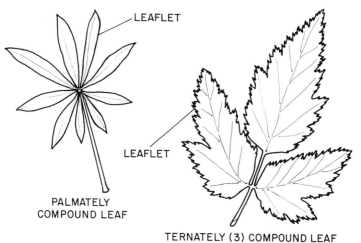

LEAFLET

LEAFLET

PALMATELY
COMPOUND LEAF

TERNATELY (3) COMPOUND LEAF

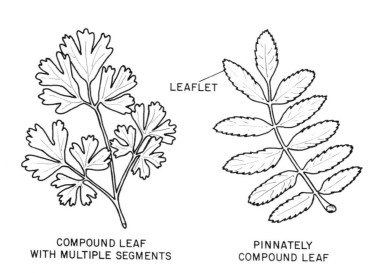

LEAFLET

COMPOUND LEAF
WITH MULTIPLE SEGMENTS

PINNATELY
COMPOUND LEAF

LEAF TYPE AND SHAPE

SIMPLE LEAVES (LEAVES NOT DIVIDED OR LOBED OR
IF SO THEN NOT DIVIDED TO THE MIDVEIN)

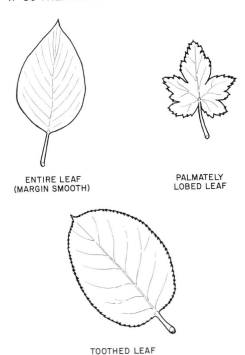

ENTIRE LEAF
(MARGIN SMOOTH)

PALMATELY
LOBED LEAF

TOOTHED LEAF

LEAF VENATION (VEIN PATTERN)

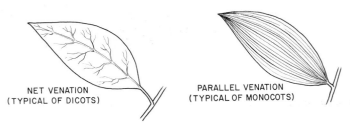

NET VENATION
(TYPICAL OF DICOTS)

PARALLEL VENATION
(TYPICAL OF MONOCOTS)

Mann

SECTION I

Continuous Forest Species
Shade Tolerant

Mixed conifer-maple forest,
Rockport State Park, near
Concrete, Washington

Cascade Aster

Douglas

Aster ledophyllus

ASTER

Aster Species—Sunflower Family

Most Asters are daisy-like plants with yellowish inner disc flowers and petal-like rays that are bluish to pink or occasionally white. Asters can usually be distinguished from daisies (*Erigeron species*) by their taller, leafy steams with several heads and their later flowering time—midsummer. They occur in subalpine meadows and open forests, often forming very dense, colorful populations.

In the Pacific Northwest there are a number of species, the most common being *Aster alpigenus* (with solitary heads), *A. foliaceus* (often with a single head), *A. ledophyllus*, and the white-rayed *A. engelmannii*. Many of the regional species are difficult to distinguish.

Stems usually several, 6-30 inches tall; leaves up to several inches long, rarely toothed, the lower often petiolate; rays 6 to numerous, pink to blue or white, approximately 1/2 inch long; disc flowers yellow; pappus of thread-like bristles. Compositae.

Taylor

ARROWLEAF BALSAMROOT

Balsamorhiza sagittata—Sunflower Family

Arrowleaf Balsamroot is a conspicuous plant with its bright-yellow, sunflower-like heads and large arrowhead-shaped leaves, the latter covered with whitish hair and borne on long leaf stalks from the root crown. It ranges from the sagebrush steppe—where it occurs in deep and fairly moist soil—into ponderosa pine forests and upward onto open, rocky ridges at mid-elevation on the eastern slopes of the Cascade Range.

In the springtime, Balsamroot provides a brilliant array of yellow along the foothills and dry ridges. The common name refers to the bitter, balsam-like taste of the woody taproot, which in spite of its distastefulness was apparently widely collected and eaten by plains Indians.

Stems several, 1-2 feet tall, leafless or bearing 1-2 reduced leaves near mid-length; leaves basal, densely silvery-hairy, long petiolate, the blade 6-12 inches long and half as wide; heads solitary and showy; rays 1-2 inches long, yellow; disc flowers yellow; pappus absent. Compositae.

Mann

BEARGRASS

Xerophyllum tenax—Lily Family

Beargrass is one of the most striking inhabitants of the forest floor, its dense, cone-shaped cluster of white flowers contrasting sharply with the forest greenery. The tall, rather coarse stems are clothed with numerous narrow, rigid leaves, particularly at the base.

Beargrass is widespread in open forests of moderately dry regions such as the eastern slopes of the Cascades and Olympics. In some areas it is extremely common and may become a dominant of the forest floor. It occurs at mid- to high elevations of the mountains, and flowers in early summer. The common name probably derives from the unpleasant, bear-like odor and grass-like leaves. It has also been called Indian Basket Grass because of having been used for basket weaving by Indians.

Stems coarse, 2-3 feet tall; leaves narrow, rigid, minutely toothed, longer and denser toward the base of the stem; flowers small in a dense, cone-shaped inflorescence which elongates with age; sepals and petals whitish, 3 each; fruit a capsule. Liliaceae.

BEARGRASS 18 Continuous

Taylor

**WILD
BLEEDINGHEART**

*Dicentra formosa
Bleedingheart Family*

Taylor

Wild Bleedingheart is a very attractive plant with its fern-like leaves and unusual flowers. The leafless stems bear several pinkish-to-purple, nodding flowers with 4 petals, 2 being conspicuous with incurved spurs at the base. The leaves, all basal, are large and divided into many small segments. The fruit is an elongate capsule which splits open at maturity releasing the numerous black, shiny seeds.

Wild Bleedingheart is common in moist lowland forests and along forest margins, occasionally extending upward to mountain meadows. Together with the Trillium, with which it is often associated, Wild Bleedingheart is among the first of the continuous forest species to flower in the spring.

Stems leafless, 8-20 inches tall; leaves divided and fern like, all basal; flowers irregular, purplish; sepals 2; petals 4, 2 small and inconspicuous, 2 showy and spurred; fruit a capsule. Fumariaceae.

Bunchberry

Mann

Bunchberry

Taylor

BUNCHBERRY

Cornus canadensis—Dogwood Family

Bunchberry or Ground Dogwood is a favorite wild flower of many outdoor enthusiasts with its attractive foliage and showy, white floral bracts (which resemble those of flowering dogwood). The woody stems creep along the ground, rooting at the nodes and producing upright branches, each with a whorl of 4 (2-6) oval, heavily veined leaves.

In moist coniferous forests—at mid-elevations in the mountains—the Bunchberry is very common and frequently covers the forest floor. It also occurs in lowland bogs. Flowers are produced in late spring, and by midsummer the attractive, edible—though not particularly palatable—red berries mature.

Low, creeping shrubs with upright branches (2-8 inches tall) and whorled, strongly veined, oval leaves; flowers small and inconspicuous, clustered in heads with 4 white, showy bracts; fruit a red berry, produced in bunches of few to several. Cornaceae.

Taylor

COLTSFOOT

Petasites frigidus — Sunflower Family

Coltsfoot grows very rapidly and flowers quickly in the early spring, thus contrasting with its drab, almost wintry surroundings. It is thick stemmed and succulent with numerous small heads of white-to-pinkish flowers. The conspicuous maple-like leaves develop after the flowers and clothe mountain roadsides throughout late spring and summer months. The seeds, like those of dandelions, are parachute like and widely scattered by the wind.

From low elevation to well up into the mountains, Coltsfoot may be found growing in very moist to wet habitats, especially along gravelly roadsides and depressions where spring runoff occurs. The plants spread by starchy rootstalks which are edible when cooked.

Flowering stems 6-24 inches tall, with heavily veined, scale-like leaves; principal leaves palmately lobed, up to 1 foot wide, derived from rhizomes; flowers mostly tubular, white or pink; pappus parachute like. Compositae.

Mann

CORAL-ROOT

Corallorhiza Species — Orchid Family

There are three rather common species of Coral-root. Striped Coral-root (*C. striata*) has pink-to-white petals with red stripes. Spotted Coral-root (*C. maculata*) has one white petal, the lower lip, with several red splotches; the other petals are reddish. Western Coral-root (*C. mertensiana*) has more uniformly reddish-brown, less colorful petals. All three flower in late spring.

Spotted Coral-root   **Striped Coral-root**

Taylor   Taylor

The reddish-brown tone of the Coral-root suggests a fungus rather than a flowering plant and, in fact, these orchids are parasitic on fungi that coat their bulbous roots. Like all non-green plants, they must draw nourishment from other living or non-living organisms. Their leaves serve no obvious function and have become small and bract like. Coral-roots can be distinguished from other non-green plants of the forest floor by their irregular (bilaterally symmetrical) flowers borne along the upper half of upright, unbranched stems. They grow in moist, dark, coniferous forests from low elevations to as high as 6,000 feet in the mountains.

Plants 8-18 inches tall, reddish brown; leaves scale like, non-green; flowers showy, reddish brown with white markings, strongly irregular; sepals 3; petals 3; ovary inferior; fruit a capsule with numerous minute seeds. Orchidaceae.

Red-flowering Currant

Mapleleaf Currant

Mann

Mann

Mann

Fruits

Prickly Currant

Flowers

Taylor

CURRANT

Ribes Species — Currant Family

As a group, Wild Currants can be recognized by their colorful sepals (as compared to petals), currant-like berries, and maple-like leaves. All are medium-sized or low shrubs with a rather strong "curranty" odor. The most common forest species is Prickly Currant (*R. lacustre*), a low, sprawling shrub thickly covered with sharp, slender prickles and larger spines. The saucer-shaped flowers are yellowish green to reddish purple and borne on drooping branches. The berries are dark purple and covered with glandular-sticky hairs. In moist habitats of the Subalpine Zone, Mapleleaf Currant (*R. howellii*) is common. It resembles Prickly Currant but has red to rust-color flowers and no spines or prickles.

Along forest streams Stink Currant (*R. bracteosum*) is common. It has larger leaves than other species and also lacks spines and prickles. Its green flowers are inconspicuous, its berries black and glandular, and it has a strong unpleasant odor. The showiest of all Northwest species is the Red-flowering Currant (*R. sanguineum*) which has pink to bright-red flowers. It is usually restricted to the lowlands, occurring on bluffs and in open forests.

Wild Currants generally grow along streams and drainages and below snow fields. All are spring-flowering plants with attractive foliage and all produce edible but sometimes non-palatable fruits.

Medium-sized, often spiny, odorous shrubs with alternate, palmately lobed leaves; flowers borne in racemes; sepals 5, showy; petals 5, small and usually inconspicuous; stamens 5; ovary inferior; fruit an edible berry. Grossulariaceae.

Taylor

DEVIL'S-CLUB

Oplopanax horridum — Ginseng Family

The yellowish thorns and spines on its stems and leaves make Devil's-club one of the most disagreeable plants of the Pacific Northwest. Yet, in spite of its armament, it is a handsome plant with large palmately lobed, maple-like leaves. Its small greenish-white flowers appear in early summer in dense, unattractive clusters. In late summer the flowers are replaced by bright-red berries. The stems may be over 10 feet tall, becoming variously twisted and distorted and often forming more or less impenetrable thickets along streams and seepage areas from the lowlands to high elevations in forests and meadows.

To the coast Indians, Devil's-club has in the past held magic power. They tied a bit of its bark to a halibut hook to insure a successful catch, and from its wood they made charms for protection against evil spirits.

Stems 3-12 feet tall, densely spiny; leaves palmately lobed, up to 12 inches wide, spiny along the petiole and veins; flowers small, borne in a spike-like inflorescence; fruit a bright-red berry. Araliaceae.

Red Elderberry in Flower

Taylor

Red Elderberry

Mann

RED ELDERBERRY

Sambucus racemosa — Honeysuckle Family

Red Elderberry is a tall shrub with soft, pithy twigs that have been widely used in making whistles. The leaves are opposite, large, and pinnately compound. The small white or cream-colored flowers occur in a pyramidal or somewhat flat-topped cluster as do the small and attractive bright-red berries.

Although more common in the lowlands, Red Elderberry extends to middle elevations and occasionally to subalpine meadows. Most commonly it grows along roadsides and forest openings. It flowers in mid-spring.

There are two species of elderberry in the Pacific Northwest, *Sambucus racemosa* and *S. caerulea* (Blue Elderberry). The latter species is more common in drier areas—such as the east slopes and foothills of the Cascade Range—and has a larger, flat-topped flower cluster. The fruits of the Blue Elderbery are, of course, blue and are widely used in preserves and wine. The fruits of the Red Elderberry, though edible, are bitter and not particularly palatable.

Shrubs 6-18 feet tall; leaves opposite, pinnately compound, with toothed leaflets; flowers whitish, 1/4 inch long, with 5 petals and 5 stamens; ovary inferior; fruit a berry. Caprifoliaceae.

Fairy-slipper

Mann

FAIRY-SLIPPER

Calypso bulbosa
Orchid Family

The beautiful flowers of the Fairy-slipper—also known as Lady-slipper and Calypso Orchid—are elegantly structured, resembling a delicate slipper. The flower color is generally lavender with white (or yellowish) markings and darker reddish spots on the lower sac-like petal. Each plant has a rather broad, parallel-veined leaf and a single fragile stem with its colorful flower.

The capsule of the Fairy-slipper—like that of other orchids—produces thousands of minute seeds which lack stored food. The germination of the seeds and subsequent establishment of the seedlings is dependent upon fungi which provide a source of nutrition. Thus, despite its many seeds, Fairy-slipper reproduces inefficiently, and indiscriminate flower picking has led to its virtual elimination from many areas where it was previously common. It now occurs sporadically from the lowlands to moderate elevation and grows in moist, humus-rich conifer forests, often hidden by the underbrush. It flowers in mid-spring.

Stems single, unbranched, 3-6 inches tall, derived from a small bulb; leaf solitary, basal, parallel veined; flowers showy, irregular; ovary inferior; fruit a many-seeded capsule. Orchidaceae.

Taylor

FALSE LILY-OF-THE-VALLEY

Maianthemum dilatatum — Lily Family

Sometimes called Wild Lily-of-the-valley or May-lily, this small but attractive sweet-smelling plant is readily identified by its unbranched upright stem and shiny heart-shaped leaves with prominent parallel veins. Rising above the 2—or occasionally 3—leaves is a slender stalk bearing small white flowers in a narrow terminal cluster. The edible red berries that follow the flowers supplemented the diet of early Northwest Indians.

False Lily-of-the-valley inhabits moist, shady sites from lowland forests to middle elevations in the mountains where it flowers in late spring. It spreads effectively by rootstalks, often forming very dense populations.

Stems 6-14 inches tall, zigzag with 2-3 bright, shiny, heart-shaped leaves; flowers white, borne in a raceme; floral parts in multiples of 4; fruit a red berry. Liliaceae.

T. unifoliata   Taylor

T. trifoliata   Taylor

FOAMFLOWER

Tiarella trifoliata
Saxifrage Family

Foamflower, or Coolwort, is an attractive inhabitant of the forest floor with its dark-green, maple-like leaves and rather weak stems crowned by an elongate cluster of delicate white flowers. It is similar in appearance to other forest plants but can be distinguished by the two unequal halves of its capsular fruit, one being about twice as large as the other. In the Northwest, there are two major forms of *Tiarella*, the more common montane form having only lobed leaves— this form often being placed in a distinct species, *T. unifoliata*—and the other form having the leaves divided into 3 leaflets.

Foamflower is one of the most widespread and abundant forest species of the Northwest, often forming a carpet with the numerous small white flowers having the fanciful appearance of foam, hence the common name. There is an extended blooming period beginning in late spring.

Stems 1 to several, 10-24 inches tall; leaves palmately lobed or divided, reduced upward on the stem; sepals 5; petals 5, very narrow, white; stamens 10; fruit a capsule with unequal halves. Saxifragaceae.

Mann

FOOL'S-HUCKLEBERRY

Menziesia ferruginea
Heath Family

As its common name implies, Fool's-huckleberry, or Mountain Azalea, may easily be confused with species of huckleberry or blueberry (*Vaccinium*). However, its leaves tend to be grouped near the ends of the branches (in this respect it resembles White Rhododendron); the tube formed by the fused petals has only 4 lobes as compared to 5 in true huckleberry; the flowers are often rust colored rather than pink; and instead of forming a berry, the ovary matures into a woody capsule, another characteristic shared with White Rhododendron.

Fool's-huckleberry is an important plant at mid- to high elevations in coniferous forests and is frequently associated with subalpine tree clumps. Occasionally it can be found growing along the border of lowland bogs. It is usually associated with huckleberries or White Rhododendron, all members of the ubiquitous Heath family (Ericaceae). It flowers in late spring.

Medium-sized shrubs; leaves ovate or elliptical, often brown hairy, clustered near the ends of branches; flowers urn shaped, yellowish to rust colored, with 4 short lobes; fruit a woody capsule. Ericaceae.

Red Foxglove

Mann

White Foxglove

Mann

FOXGLOVE

Digitalis purpurea — Figwort Family

Few plants can rival Foxglove for floral beauty. The petals vary in color from white to dark red or purple—usually with darker spots—and are fused into an attractive tubular structure with the lower part of the petals extended outward, lip like, serving as a landing platform for pollinators.

Foxglove is an introduced biennial which is now widely established in waste areas and along roadsides, extending to mid-elevations in the mountains. The first year it exists as a clump or rosette of rather large, toothed, densely hairy leaves. The second year, tall leafy stems are produced which bear flowers in late spring and early summer. This species is the source of the heart drug, digitalis.

Stems tall (up to 6 feet), coarse, unbranched; leaves up to 1 foot long, half as wide, densely hairy, toothed, reduced in size upward on the stem; flowers irregular, tubular, 1-2 inches long, borne in a 1-sided raceme; fruit a capsule. Scrophulariaceae.

FOXGLOVE 32 Continuous

Taylor   Taylor

FRINGECUP

Tellima grandiflora — Saxifrage Family

The flowers of Fringecup are very unusual. The sepals are greenish and form a rather broad, cup-like tube; and the conspicuously fringed petals are greenish white to reddish, extending outward and backward over the top of the sepal tube. The resulting impression is that of a fringed cup. The plants are hairy and rather tall with weak stems and roundish maple-like leaves. The flowers are borne in a row along the upper part of the stem.

Fringecup grows along stream banks and other moist sites in open forests and forest margins from low elevations to the Subalpine Zone. It is also common along the sides of mountain trails. It flowers in mid-spring.

Stems several, weak, hairy, 2-3 feet tall; leaves palmately lobed, round in outline, mostly basal (being reduced upward on the stem) with long, hairy petioles; sepals 5, green; petals 5, green to red, fringed, spreading or bent backward; fruit a capsule. Saxifragaceae.

Mann

WILD GINGER

Asarum caudatum — Dutchman's Pipe Family

Wild Ginger is a creeping plant with broad heart-shaped leaves that often form carpets over the moist forest floor. The flowers have an unusual coloration of brownish purple and, though rather large, easily escape detection hidden among the dark, velvety leaves and camouflaged against the brown-black organic soil.

Populations of Wild Ginger occur occasionally in very moist, shady sites of conifer forests—mostly at middle elevations in the mountains. Flowers appear in early summer.

Wild Ginger is a fragrant and spicy plant used extensively by the wild-plant gourmet in the preparation of a number of foods, candies, and beverages. The plants have also been cultivated as an attractive ground cover.

Low fragrant herbs which spread by runners or rhizomes; leaves in pairs, heart-shaped, 2-4 inches long, 3-5 inches wide; sepals brownish purple, up to 3 inches long with an elongate thread-like tip; petals none; fruit a fleshy capsule. Aristolochiaceae.

Goatsbeard

Ocean Spray

Taylor

GOATSBEARD

Aruncus sylvester
Rose Family

Taylor

The large, somewhat fern-like leaves and showy spray-like flower clusters of Goatsbeard combine to make it a very attractive plant. It is a tall, extensively branched herb with many large leaves divided into several toothed leaflets, each resembling a single leaf. The flowers, which appear in late spring, are white and small but very numerous in the flexuous, branched cluster.

Goatsbeard is common at low to moderate elevations on the west side of the Pacific ranges. It is usually found in moist, open forests or along the forest edge, but is also common on sparsely forested ridges and may extend into mountain meadows, particularly in gravelly sites. The related Ocean Spray (*Holodiscus discolor*) has similar flowers and spray-like flower clusters but is a large shrub with undivided, coarsely toothed leaves and is more or less restricted to the foothills.

Stems several, 3-6 feet tall, often woody at the base; leaves twice pinnately compound with long petioles and sharply toothed, ovate leaflets; flowers small, white, unisexual, the male (pollen producing) larger and showier, the female producing 2-5 few-seeded, dehiscent fruits. Rosaceae.

Mountain Huckleberry

Taylor

Oval-leaf Huckleberry

Taylor

Mann

HUCKLEBERRY

Vaccinium Species — Heath Family

Huckleberries, or Blueberries, are conspicuous and important plants throughout the northern and montane conifer forests of North America. In the Pacific Northwest the three most common forest species are Red Huckleberry (*Vaccinium parvifolium*), Mountain Huckleberry (*V. membranaceum*), and Oval-leaf Huckleberry (*V. ovalifolium*). All three are low to medium-sized shrubs with alternate leaves and white-to-pinkish, urn-shaped flowers.

Red Huckleberry is more common in the lower forests, particularly in logged or burned areas and along roadsides, often growing from rotting stumps or logs. The stems and branches are green and prominently angled with numerous small, bright-green, oval-shaped leaves. The attractive bright-red berries are tart but have an excellent flavor, especially when made into wine or pie.

Oval-leaf Huckleberry has yellowish-to-gray, angled branches, with late-developing, oval, dull-green leaves. The berries are purple but have a blue coating. Although bland tasting, they make excellent pies and preserves. This is the most common species at mid-elevations.

Mountain Huckleberry occurs in the upper montane forests and invades previously logged areas, where the plants often produce a heavy crop of relatively large, deep-purple, delicious berries. The leaves are sharp pointed, toothed, and are longer than those of other species.

Small to medium-sized shrubs; leaves alternate, sometimes toothed, not clustered near the branch tips; flowers white to pink, urn shaped with 5 lobes; ovary inferior; fruit an edible berry. Ericaceae.

Indian-pipe

Taylor

INDIAN-PIPE

Monotropa uniflora — Heath Family

Indian-pipe is one of the most unusual plants of the Pacific Northwest, being entirely chalky white. The clustered stems are thick and succulent with scale-like leaves and solitary nodding flowers. Each stem with its flower resembles a long, inverted pipe.

Like other non-green plants, Indian-pipe cannot carry on photosynthesis but must get energy from some external organic source. The source in this case is fungi which in turn derive their nutrition from digestion of organic material of the forest floor and from the roots of trees such as Douglas Fir.

Indian-pipe is an occasional inhabitant of dark, moist woods from low to middle elevations. It flowers in midsummer.

Stems several, 1/2 inch thick and 6-18 inches tall, white (aging or drying black) with scale-like leaves; flowers solitary, nodding, white, with 5 sepals, 5 petals, and 10 stamens; ovary superior; fruit a capsule. Ericaceae.

Taylor

INDIAN-PLUM

Osmaronia cerasiformis — Rose Family

In early spring, Indian-plum—a medium-sized or large shrub—is very conspicuous in the forest community because it produces leaves and flowers earlier than most associated plants. The leaves are elliptical, smooth margined, and usually clustered near the ends of the branches. The flowers are white and hang in loose clusters from branch tips. The fruits are plum like and edible but can seldom be collected because they ripen slowly and are quickly eaten by birds.

Unisexual shrubs up to 10 feet tall, with alternate, elliptical, non-toothed leaves; flowers of staminate (male) plants with numerous stamens, those of the pistillate plant with 2-5 ovaries—each maturing into a plum-like fruit—and many small non-functional stamens; sepals 5; petals 5, white. Rosaceae.

Sorbus scopulina   Taylor

MOUNTAIN-ASH

Sorbus Species — Rose Family

Mountain-ash is an attractive shrub with its large, pinnately compound leaves and dense, flat-topped cluster of white flowers that give rise to red-orange berries. The berries are edible and regularly eaten by birds, often resulting in mild intoxication. In the Pacific Northwest there are two variable species of Mountain-ash, *S. scopulina* with sharp-pointed, shallow-toothed leaflets, and *S. sitchensis* with rounder, more deeply toothed leaflets.

Mountain-ash frequently occurs in open forests and logged areas. Occasionally it extends upward into the Subalpine Zone, where it grows in meadows and is associated with tree clumps. It is now widely cultivated for its beauty and hardiness.

Medium-sized shrubs or small trees with alternate, pinnately compound leaves and toothed leaflets; flowers white, in a dense, flat-topped cluster; sepals 5; petals 5; stamens numerous; fruit a reddish berry. Rosaceae.

Taylor

Tall Oregon-grape

Taylor

OREGON-GRAPE

Berberis Species
Barberry Family

Oregon-grape is clearly distinguished by its shiny evergreen leaves —with spiny, holly-like leaflets—and bright-yellow, fragrant flowers that are produced in one or more elongate clusters at the tips of short, shrubby stems. The fruits develop into purple berries with a blue coating.

There are two species of Oregon-grape in the Pacific Northwest, Cascade Oregon-grape (*Berberis nervosa*) and Tall Oregon-grape (*B. aquifolium*). The former is a low, unbranched shrub occurring from the lowlands to medium elevations in relatively dry sites, where it is often a dominant associate of Douglas Fir. *Berberis aquifolium*, a taller (up to 6 feet) shrub with a shorter and denser flower cluster, occurs in open forests and forest margins of the lowlands. Both species flower early in the spring and produce edible but tart berries which make excellent preserves or wine.

Low to medium-sized shrubs (1-6 feet); leaves pinnately compound, evergreen; leaflets 5-9 (*B. aquifolium*) or 11-19 (*B. nervosa*), spiny along the margin; flowers yellow, parts in multiples of 3; fruit an edible berry. Berberidaceae.

Oxeye-daisy

Taylor

OXEYE-DAISY

Chrysanthemum leucanthemum
Sunflower Family

Oxeye-daisy is well marked by its large, solitary, daisy-like head—with white rays and a yellow center—and deeply toothed or lobed leaves. It is conspicuous along roadsides, in fields, and in waste areas; hence, it is well known throughout the Pacific Northwest.

Oxeye-daisy is most abundant at low elevations but may extend upward to moderate elevations in suitable habitats. It flowers throughout early summer, and though an attractive and long-lived cut-flower plant, it unfortunately has an unpleasant odor.

Stems unbranched, 10-30 inches tall; leaves lobed or deeply toothed, the lower ones petiolate; heads solitary; rays white, approximately 1/2 inch long; disc flowers yellow; pappus absent. Compositae.

Taylor

Mann

PEARLY-EVERLASTING

Anaphalis margaritacea — Sunflower Family

The individual flowers of Pearly-everlasting are minute and grouped into small heads, each surrounded by several pearly-white, papery bracts. The bracts and flowers retain their shape and attractive color even after the plants have been dried—hence the common name. The stems and elongate leaves are covered with white, woolly hair.

Pearly-everlasting is not a true forest species but occurs along roadsides and in other gravelly, disturbed areas within the confines of the Continuous Forest Zone, from sea level to approximately 5,000 feet. It flowers during the summer months.

Plants white-woolly, 1-3 feet tall, unbranched below the inflorescence, rhizomatous; leaves narrow, 2-4 inches long with a prominent mid-vein, non-toothed, equally distributed along the stem; rays absent; disc flowers yellow; bracts of the numerous heads pearly white. Compositae.

Pinesap

Mann

Candystick

Mann

PINESAP

Hypopitys monotropa and Related Species — Heath Family

Pinesap, or Fringed-pinesap, is an unusual, yellowish-brown or pinkish inhabitant of the humus-rich forest floor. Its succulent stems are generally less than 6 inches tall and arc downward until long after the flowers are produced, eventually elongating and becoming erect. The leaves are scale like.

Of the several non-green members of the Heath (Ericaceae) family, Pinesap is the most common in the Pacific Northwest, but by no means the most conspicuous. Three additional species include Candystick (*Allotropa virgata*), a plant usually less than 18 inches tall with alternating white and pink stripes, many scale-like, pinkish-brown leaves, and similarly colored flowers with conspicuous purple-tipped stamens; Woodland-pinedrops (*Pterospora andromedea*), a tall (up to 3 feet), coarse, and sticky reddish-brown plant with a few bracts and several pale-yellow, nodding flowers; and Indian-pipe (*Monotropa uniflora*), described separately under that name.

These and other members of the Heath family which lack green tissue are, of course, non-photosynthetic. This has its advantages, however, since the plants can grow in the deep shade of moist forests where the growth of light-requiring green plants is inhibited. These non-green plants have an interesting relationship with fungi, from which they derive their nutrition and water. They flower during the summer months.

Pond-lily

Taylor

Taylor

POND-LILY

Nuphar polysepalum
Water-lily Family

The Pond-lily is distinctive because of its broad, floating leaves ("lily pads") and large yellow flowers. Both flowers and leaves are buoyed up by trapped air and are borne on long stalks derived from starchy, edible, underground stems (rhizomes). Each of the 2-inch flowers has a broad, "scalloped" pollen-receptive stigma, numerous reddish-yellow stamens, and several fleshy yellow or reddish petals.

The Pond-lily is an attractive inhabitant of bogs, marshes, shallow ponds, and lake shores, from the lowlands to medium elevations.

Aquatic herbs with floating, broadly heart-shaped leaves (6-18 inches long and nearly as wide) and large yellow flowers (2 inches in diameter); flower stalks and leaf petioles elongate and derived from underground rhizomes. Nymphaeaceae.

POND-LILY 46 Continuous

Mann

PRINCE'S-PINE

Chimaphila umbellata — Heath Family

Prince's-pine, or Pipsissewa, can easily be recognized by its elongate, toothed, evergreen leaves which occur in one or more whorls along the short stem. The flowers are pale (nearly white) to dark rose and nod in an umbrella-like cluster (umbel) at the top of the stem. A similar species, *C. menziesii*, has opposite leaves and fewer flowers. The two species overlap in distribution.

Prince's-pine is a frequent inhabitant of moist, coniferous forests, and in many sites, particularly in deep shade, it becomes an understory dominant. The flowering period is late spring and early summer.

Stems unbranched, 4-10 inches tall, woody at the base; leaves evergreen, narrow, toothed, 1-3 inches long, borne in 1-2 whorls on the stem; flowers nodding in an umbel; sepals 5; petals 5, pinkish; stamens 10; fruit a capsule. Ericaceae.

Taylor

QUEEN'S-CUP

Clintonia uniflora — Lily Family

Queen's-cup is one of the most distinctive and beautiful mountain flowers of the Northwest. Its attractive white flowers are solitary on short leafless stalks and resemble shallow cups or upright bells. The 2 or 3 leaves—which are leathery, strap-like, and shiny—are derived from underground stems. The fruit is a blue berry of questionable edibility.

Queen's-cup is widely distributed in hemlock-silver fir forests at middle and high elevations. It flowers in early summer.

Plants stemless, the flower stalk and leaves derived from fleshy, fibrous roots; leaves 2-3, leathery, strap like, shiny, parallel veined; flowers white, 1 to 1-1/2 inches across; sepals and petals similar, 3 each; fruit a blue berry. Liliaceae.

Valum

RATTLESNAKE-PLANTAIN

Goodyera oblongifolia — Orchid Family

The most characteristic and noticeable feature of Rattlesnake-plantain is the interesting coloration of its leaves, which are borne in a whorl or rosette on or near the ground. They are dark green with distinctive white stripes or splotches, especially along the mid-vein—hence the common name. The small, dull-white flowers are irregular (bilaterally symmetrical) and are produced in a long cluster at the tip of the solitary leafless stem.

Rattlesnake-plantain occurs sporadically over a wide range of coniferous forest habitats from low to rather high elevations. Flowers are produced in late summer.

Stems single, unbranched, leafless; leaves basal, white striped or mottled; flowers small, dull white, irregular, borne in a dense raceme; ovary inferior; fruit a capsule. Orchidaceae.

Mann

PACIFIC RHODODENDRON

Rhododendron macrophyllum — Heath Family

Pacific (or Western) Rhododendron is one of the most attractive plants of the Northwest and has the distinction of being the state flower of Washington. A medium-sized, evergreen shrub, its dark-green leathery leaves set off the clusters of large, pale-pink-to-purplish, broadly bell-shaped flowers which occur at the ends of the branches.

Pacific Rhododendron inhabits conifer forests and forest margins along the west side of the Cascades and Olympics from Canada to California. It is frequently cultivated and has become a familiar and favorite spring flowering shrub for many West Coast residents.

Evergreen shrubs, 3-12 feet tall; leaves non-toothed, leathery, elliptical, 3-8 inches long; flowers pink to purple, 2 inches across, with 5 spreading petals; ovary superior; fruit a woody capsule. Ericaceae.

Mann

WHITE RHODODENDRON

Rhododendron albiflorum — Heath Family

Though easily recognized by its showy flowers, White Rhododendron closely resembles other members of the Heath family, especially Fool's-huckleberry (*Menziesia ferruginea*). It is a rather tall shrub, with whorls of 5 to 7 elliptical leaves near the tips of the branches. Flowers are white to cream colored, broadly bell shaped, and occur in clusters along the stem.

White Rhododendron is fairly common in moist forests at high elevations, particularly in areas of deep snow accumulation. It also occurs along the edges of subalpine tree clumps where it often forms dense thickets. It flowers in early summer.

Shrubs, 3-7 feet tall; leaves alternate (but grouped at the branch ends), elliptical, 2-4 inches long; flowers white, approximately 1 inch wide; sepals 5; petals 5; fruit a woody capsule. Ericaceae.

Taylor

SALAL

Gaultheria shallon — Heath Family

Salal is a low to medium-sized shrub easily identified by its ever-green and leathery oval leaves with conspicuous veins. White-to-pink, urn-shaped flowers hanging in clusters from the tips of the many leafy branches add to the general attractiveness of the plant. The dark-purple berries were often gathered and eaten by Indians and early settlers and are still a major source of food for many animals. The stems, flowers, and berries are loosely covered by glandular-sticky hairs.

Salal is very common in relatively dry habitats—especially in Douglas Fir forests—from the coast to mid-elevations. It flowers in late spring.

Much-branched, low-to-medium-sized, glandular-hairy shrub; leaves evergreen, leathery, strongly veined, ovate, 2-4 inches long and half as wide; flowers white to pink, urn shaped, pendent; fruit a purple, edible berry. Ericaceae.

Mann

Taylor

SALMONBERRY

Rubus spectabilis — Rose Family

Salmonberry can be recognized in all seasons by its chestnut-brown, sparsely-spiny stems with their crooked or zigzag shape. The inner tissue of the stems is soft, starchy, and edible. The leaves are divided into 3 leaflets—each coarsely toothed—and the attractive flowers are pink to red. The raspberry-like fruits are yellow orange (salmon colored) or red and, although somewhat bland, are edible and can be made into good wine.

A common shrub, extending from lowlands to mid-elevations in the mountains, Salmonberry occurs along roadsides and creeks and in forest openings and logged areas, often forming dense thickets. It flowers over a period of several weeks, beginning early in spring.

Stems woody, often spiny, 5-8 feet tall; leaves compound with 3 toothed leaflets; sepals 5; petals 5, pink to red, 1/2 inch long; stamens numerous; fruit raspberry like, red or salmon colored. Rosaceae.

SIBERIAN MINER'S-LETTUCE

Montia sibirica — Purslane Family

Siberian Miner's-lettuce, or Candyflower, is a succulent plant with many weak, spreading stems bearing delicate flowers with white or pink petals and darker pink stripes. The basal leaves have long leaf stalks with a somewhat triangular blade. Only 2 leaves are borne on the stem; these are opposite, lack petioles, and occur just below the flower cluster. This plant is common in moist, shady sites, especially in the lowlands. It flowers in mid-spring and can be eaten much like lettuce.

Stems several, spreading, succulent, brittle, bearing 2 opposite leaves below the inflorescence; leaves mostly basal, long petiolate, with elliptical blades; sepals 2; petals 5, white to pink, striped; fruit a capsule with black, shiny seeds. Portulacaceae.

SKUNK-CABBAGE

Mann

Lysichitum americanum
Arum Family

In late winter or early spring, the attractive bright-yellow, modified leaf (spathe) of Skunk-cabbage appears in wet, boggy, forested or open places. Ensheathed by the spathe is a thick, fleshy stem terminated by a dense cluster (spadix) of yellow-green flowers. The large green leaves develop later. The plant gets its name from the cabbage-like leaves and characteristic skunky smell that attracts pollinating flies. Leaves and roots are edible but only after being boiled several times to remove irritants.

Stems 1 to few, thick, fleshy, 8-24 inches tall, terminated by a spadix of small, yellow-green flowers, ensheathed by a yellow spathe; leaves 1-3 feet, half as wide, developing after the spathe and flowers. Araceae.

Taylor

Mann

SOLOMON-SEAL

Smilacina Species
Lily Family

There are two species of *Smilacina* in the Pacific Northwest—Star-flowered Solomon-seal (Smilacina stellata) and False Solomon-seal (*S. racemosa*). Both have alternate, bright, glossy-green leaves with conspicuous parallel veins. Their flowers are creamy white, with those of False Solomon-seal being individually smaller but much more numerous and borne in a dense, branched cluster at the stem tip. The 10 or fewer flowers of *S. stellata* are somewhat star shaped and borne along the unbranched, zigzag stem tip. The berries of the Star-flowered Solomon-seal are greenish yellow, becoming black, while those of the False Solomon-seal are red. Both are edible when ripe.

Both species occur in open, moist forests or meadow areas with *S. stellata* extending higher into the mountains. Both flower in mid- to late spring.

Stems unbranched, 1-3 feet tall, rhizomatous; leaves ovate (narrower in *S. stellata*), 4-8 inches long, bright green, strongly parallel veined, clasping the stem; flowers white; sepals and petals similar, 3 each, 1/4 inch long (less in *S. racemosa*); fruit a berry. Liliaceae.

Valum

Subalpine Forest with autumn coloration of Huckleberry and Mountain-ash. Mt. Shuksan is in background.

Mann

SPIRAEA

Spiraea Species — Rose Family

Spiraeas are low to medium-sized shrubs with dense, showy clusters of very small flowers and alternate, toothed leaves. In the Pacific Northwest, there are three common species, their differences being in flower color, and shape of the flower cluster (inflorescence).

The most common lowland species, Douglas Spiraea (*Spiraea douglasii*), has pink-to-red flowers in elongate, pyramidal inflorescences. It occasionally extends upward into subalpine meadows. The most widespread montane species is Subalpine Spiraea (*Spiraea densiflora*) with pink-to-red, flat-topped inflorescences. It occurs in open forests at high elevations or along the forest margins in subalpine meadows. The white-flowered Birch-leaf Spiraea (*Spiraea betulifolia*) is common in dry, montane forests such as in the Rocky Mountains and Eastern Cascades. All species flower during the summer months.

Low to medium-sized shrubs; leaves alternate, toothed at the base; flowers small in dense inflorescences; sepals 5; petals 5; stamens numerous; fruits small, few-seeded follicles. Rosaceae.

Taylor

WESTERN STARFLOWER

Trientalis latifolia — Primrose Family

Western Starflower can easily be recognized by the whorl of 4 to 8 broadly elliptical leaves above which the 2 to several white or pink star-shaped flowers are derived on thread-like stalks (pedicels). Each plant is single stemmed and has a bulbous root.

Western Starflower is an attractive plant that occurs at all elevations from sea level to subalpine meadows. It is most common in moist, rather open forests but may be found in meadows formed along avalanche tracks. It flowers in late spring.

Stems unbranched, 4-6 inches tall, bearing a single whorl of 4-8 leaves, otherwise leafless; flowers white, sepals, petals, and stamens 6 (5-7); fruit a capsule. Primulaceae.

Taylor

STRAWBERRY-BRAMBLE

Rubus pedatus — Rose Family

Strawberry-bramble is a low, trailing plant which closely resembles wild strawberry but can easily be distinguished by its woody runners and palmately divided leaves with 5 leaflets rather than the characteristic 3 of strawberries. Also, although the flowers of both species are similar in size, color, and other aspects, the fruits are very different. Each bramble flower produces 1 to several (usually 2) hard but edible red "berries."

Strawberry-bramble is common in moist, montane forests, often forming extensive, attractive carpets. It also reaches into the Subalpine Zone where it is often associated with tree clumps. A closely related species, *Rubus lasiococcus*—with palmately lobed rather than divided leaves—has similar ecological requirements but generally a more southerly distribution. Both species flower in late spring.

Low, trailing plants with woody runners; leaves palmately compound with 5 leaflets (*R. pedatus*) or palmately lobed (*R. lasiococcus*); flowers white, strawberry like; sepals 5; petals 5; stamens numerous; fruit 1 to several 1-seeded "berries." Rosaceae.

Thimbleberry

Thimbleberry

Taylor

Mann

THIMBLEBERRY

Rubus parviflorus — Rose Family

Thimbleberry is an easily recognized and attractive shrub with showy white flowers that contrast sharply against the background of large, dark-green, maple-like leaves. The fruits mature into scarlet-red, thimble-like "berries," which are considered a delicacy by many people.

This shrub is widespread in the Northwest, occurring from the lowlands to the Subalpine Zone. It is especially common in forest openings and along streams at lower elevations. It is also conspicuous along avalanche tracks and other rocky meadow areas. The flowers are produced in late spring.

Medium-sized, non-spiny shrubs; leaves dark green, alternate, palmately lobed, 4-8 inches wide; flowers white, 2 inches across; sepals 5; petals 5; stamens numerous; fruit red, thimble shaped, and raspberry like, edible. Rosaceae.

THIMBLEBERRY 62 Continuous

Taylor

TRAIL-PLANT

Adenocaulon bicolor — Sunflower Family

Trail-plant is recognized by its leaves and not by its minute white flowers—which are borne in small heads on short, thin branches along the upper half or third of the weak stem. The leaves are rather large, conspicuously veined, and triangle shaped. They are produced near the base of the plant and arranged so that the flat sides are parallel to the earth. The upper and lower surfaces of these attractive leaves contrast sharply, the upper being dark green, the lower white with dense, woolly hairs. The common name relates to the fact that if someone or something passes through an area where the plant occurs, the leaves are disoriented, thus showing their contrasting sides and marking the path taken by the "trespasser."

Trail-plant is common in moist forests from sea level to mid-elevations in the mountains. It achieves its full growth in late spring and flowers soon thereafter.

Stems thin and flexuous, unbranched below the inflorescence; leaves 2-6 inches long and wide, heart or triangle shaped, veined, dark green above and woolly white below; rays none, disc flowers minute, 10-15 in small heads; pappus none. Compositae.

Taylor

TRILLIUM

Trillium ovatum — Lily Family

The Trillium, or Wake-robin, is a conspicuous and well-known plant. The stem grows to about 1 foot in height and supports a whorl of 3 net-veined leaves that form a "cradle" for a single large flower. The 3 showy petals are snow white, aging to purple or pink as in above photo. The flowers are long lasting and pleasantly fragrant.

From the lowlands to rather high elevations in the mountains, one of the first signs of spring is the appearance of the beautiful Trillium. It occurs in shady forest habitats that are usually kept moist by melting snow at the time the Trillium flowers.

Stems succulent, 6-12 inches tall; leaves broadly ovate, net veined, in a single whorl of 3; sepals 3, green; petals 3, white, aging to pink purple; fruit a fleshy capsule. Liliaceae.

Heart-leafed Twayblade

Western Twayblade

Taylor

Taylor

TWAYBLADE

Listera Species — Orchid Family

The small, fragile Twayblades usually escape notice in their shady, moist forest environment. Their flowers are small and inconspicuous with greenish-to-brown petals. In the Heart-leafed Twayblade (*L. cordata*) the lower petal is forked; in the Western Twayblade (*L. caurina*) it is flat and elongate. All Twayblades have a single pair of ovate or heart-shaped, heavily veined leaves which gave rise to their common name, "twa," an early form of two.

Orchids are usually thought of as large, beautiful, and exotic. Twayblades are none of these; yet they are orchid like in their floral structure. The smallest and most common of four Northwest species is *L. cordata*, which often grows with moss along the top of decaying logs. All species flower in the springtime.

Stems fragile, unbranched, 2-6 inches tall; leaves 2, opposite, ovate or heart shaped, bright green, heavily veined; flowers small, green or brownish, irregular; ovary inferior; fruit a capsule. Orchidaceae.

Twinflower

Taylor   Taylor

TWINFLOWER

Linnaea borealis — Honeysuckle Family

Twinflower is a low-trailing shrub that forms shiny green carpets over the dark forest floor. Its attractive evergreen leaves occur in pairs on short upright branches. The delicate flowers are pink to lavender, hanging like bells, in pairs, from the branched tip of upright stems.

Twinflower is widely distributed in the Northwest, both geographically and altitudinally. It was named in honor of the famous 18th Century Swedish Botanist, Carolus Linnaeus.

Low-trailing shrubs with opposite, toothed, evergreen leaves; flowers bell shaped, nodding; petals lavender, fused, with 5 lobes; ovary inferior; fruit 1-seeded. Caprifoliaceae.

Taylor

ROSY

TWISTED-STALK

Streptopus roseus
Lily Family

The stems and leaves of Rosy Twisted-stalk closely resemble those of Solomon-seal (*Smilacina* species), both having erect, rather succulent stems with many large, ovate, bright-green parallel-veined leaves. However, the pinkish-to-lavender flowers of Rosy Twisted-stalk are bell shaped and borne singly on stalks from leaf bases. This and the white-flowered Clasping-leaved Twisted-stalk (*Streptopus amplexifolius*) derive their common name from the twisting of the flower stalks in such a way that the flowers appear to be produced on only the lower side of the stem.The fruit is a bright red translucent berry.

Rosy Twisted-stalk is a common and attractive plant of moist hemlock-fir forests at middle and high elevations. It flowers in early summer.

Plants erect, mostly unbranched, 1-2 feet tall, rhizomatous; leaves ovate, 2-4 inches long, bright green, parallel veined; flowers bell shaped, solitary on twisted pedicels; petals and sepals rose purple, 3 each; fruit a berry. Liliaceae.

Vanilla-leaf

Taylor

Taylor

VANILLA-LEAF

Achlys triphylla
Barberry Family

Vanilla-leaf is well marked by its single large leaf with 3 wedge-shaped or fan-shaped leaflets. The leaf is borne on a long stalk (petiole) derived from an underground rootstalk (rhizome). Also derived from the rhizome is the solitary stem, somewhat taller than the leaf and often extending upward between the leaflets. The small, white flowers lack sepals and petals and occur in a dense spike-like cluster.

Vanilla-leaf is certainly one of the most conspicuous and easily recognized herbs of moist and shady hemlock-fir forests, where its broad leaves often cover large areas. It flowers in late spring and derives its name from the vanilla-like smell of the leaves when dried and crushed.

Stems solitary, unbranched, 1-2 feet tall, rhizomatous; leaf solitary on a long petiole, basal, compound with 3 wedge-shaped leaflets; flowers without sepals and petals, borne in dense terminal spikes; stamens several, white; fruit a berry. Berberidaceae.

Pioneer Violet

Taylor

Evergreen Violet

Taylor

VIOLET

Viola Species — Violet Family

Although there are blue violets in the Pacific Northwest—for example, the common Blue Violet (*Viola adunca*), an occasional plant of montane meadows, and Marsh Violet (*V. palustris*), a small-flowered bog species—most violets have yellow flowers easily recognized by their pansy-like appearance.

The Pioneer or Wood Violet (*Viola glabella*) is the tallest, most common, and most easily identified of the Northwest species. Its stems are up to 1 foot tall and bear, near their tip, 2 or more bright-green, heart-shaped leaves. The flowers are bright yellow with thin purple-to-brownish lines, particularly on the lower petals. The Pioneer Violet grows in open montane forests and subalpine meadows where its brilliant color is a herald of spring.

The Evergreen Violet (*V. sempervirens*) is an equally attractive yellow-flowered species of the continuous forest. It is a low-spreading plant with shiny, heart-shaped leaves. A similar woodland species is the Round-leaf Violet (*V. orbiculata*) which has larger and rounder leaves and lacks runners. All three yellow violets flower almost immediately after the withdrawal of snow.

Stems erect and tall (*V. glabella*), or low (*V. orbiculata*), or low and spreading with runners (*V. sempervirens*); leaves mostly heart shaped; flowers irregular; sepals 5; petals 5, yellow (or blue white); fruit an explosive capsule. Violaceae.

Pink Wintergreen

One-sided Wintergreen

Mann

Mann

WINTERGREEN

Pyrola Species — Heath Family

Wintergreens are rather attractive evergreen shrubs which grow in shady, moist habitats of montane forests. All are low plants—seldom more than 1 foot tall—with woody runners or rootstalks (rhizomes) and mostly basal, often reddish-mottled leaves. The nodding flowers range in color from greenish white to purplish red and tend to be flattened from top to bottom.

The showiest of the Wintergreens is Pink Wintergreen (*Pyrola asarifolia*) with its colorful purplish-red flowers and broad, dark-green mottled leaves. The most widespread species is One-sided Wintergreen (*P. secunda*) with a row of greenish-white flowers and several bright green leaves which extend nearly halfway up the stem. These and other species flower during the summer.

Low evergreen, unbranched shrubs, spreading by runners or rhizomes; leaves mostly basal, ovate, or heart shaped, often toothed; flowers nodding, flattened, borne in racemes; sepals and petals 5; stamens 10; fruit a capsule. Ericaceae.

Taylor

Taylor

YOUTH-ON-AGE

Tolmiea menziesii — Saxifrage Family

When young, Youth-on-age is easily mistaken for Foamflower or Fringecup (and vice versa), all having soft-hairy stems and petioles (leaf stalks) and maple-like leaves. However, the flowers of Youth-on-age are readily distinguished by their greenish-purple to chocolate-colored sepals and very narrow (linear) chocolate-colored petals. Also, Youth-on-age is unique in that it reproduces vegetatively by the development of buds and young plants at the base of leaf blades— hence its common name.

Like Foamflower, Youth-on-age is common in moist, shady habitats, occasionally invading open areas. It ranges from the lowlands to moderate elevations and flowers in late spring.

Stems several, unbranched, soft hairy, 1 to 2-1/2 feet tall, spreading by rootstalks; leaves palmately lobed, mostly basal, soft hairy (especially the long petioles); flowers small, green-chocolate, borne in racemes; sepals 5; petals 5, linear and inconspicuous; fruit a capsule. Saxifragaceae.

Mann

SECTION II

Subalpine and Alpine Species

Subalpine meadow on Skyline Divide with
Mount Baker in the background.

Subalpine Meadow in Mount Rainier National Park showing lupine with scattered tree clumps in background.

ORANGE AGOSERIS

Agoseris aurantiaca — Sunflower Family

To many people the Orange Agoseris (or Mountain Dandelion), with its unusual coloration, is among the most attractive of our mountain wild flowers. The heads closely resemble those of dandelion but have burnt-orange colored rays. Like the dandelion, the seeds have a parachute-like pappus and are scattered by the wind. The leaves are all basal and are lobed or toothed.

The Orange Agoseris is fairly common in moist subalpine meadows and avalanche tracks. It occurs more often in suitable lush meadow habitats than is realized because the flowers close early on hot, sunny days and the plants become "hidden" among the associated vegetation.

Stems unbranched, leafless, woolly hairy, 6-12 inches tall; leaves basal, usually toothed or lobed, narrow and several inches long; heads solitary, approximately 1 inch wide; rays burnt orange, sometimes pink or purple (especially with age); disc flowers none; pappus parachute like. Compositae.

Western Anemone in Flower

Western Anemone in Fruit

Taylor

WESTERN ANEMONE

Anemone occidentalis — Buttercup Family

The Western Anemone, or Western Windflower (anemone means wind), has a characteristic shaggy head of several one-seeded fruits (achenes)—each with a long, feathery style that helps the wind scatter the seeds. The showy white, or bluish, flowers are borne singly on low, hairy stems that elongate considerably as the fruits mature. The leaves are large and fern like. The plant is common in moist mountain meadows of the Subalpine Zone and one of the first to flower in spring.

Drummond's Anemone (*A. drummondii*), a similar species, occurs in the Alpine Zone, mostly on moist, gravelly slopes, but is about half the size, has blue flowers, and lacks the feathery styles.

Stems unbranched, densely hairy, 1-2 feet tall in fruit, much shorter in flower; leaves finely divided and fern like; flowers 1-2 inches wide, white or bluish; sepals 5-7, petals none; stamens numerous; achenes numerous, with feathery styles when mature. Ranunculaceae.

Meadow ANEMONE 79

Broadleaf Arnica

Nevada Arnica

Taylor

Taylor

BROADLEAF ARNICA

Arnica latifolia — Sunflower Family

The various arnicas can be distinguished from other yellow-flowered members of the sunflower family by their opposite rather than alternate leaves. In addition to Broadleaf Arnica (*A. latifolia*) there are several alpine or subalpine species such as Nevada Arnica (*A. nevadensis*). There is also one notable forest species, Heartleaf Arnica (*A. cordifolia*) which has broad, heart-shaped leaves and showy sunflower-like heads. It is common in the Rocky Mountains and occurs in the drier forests of the eastern Cascades.

Broadleaf Arnica is taller than most other arnicas and has more stem leaves, 3 to 5 pairs, the upper ones reduced in size. It is one of the most common inhabitants of subalpine meadow communities where it contributes to the spectacular summer coloration.

Stems unbranched, 1-2 feet tall, derived from rhizomes; leaves ovate to heart shaped, sharply toothed, 1 to several inches long and half as wide, 3-5 pairs per stem; heads yellow, few per stem, with both rays and disc flowers; pappus of hair-like bristles. Compositae.

Taylor

BELLFLOWER

Campanula rotundifolia
Bellflower Family

The showy Bellflower is easily recognized by its blue petals which are fused into a bell-shaped tube with 5 triangular lobes. The regular flowers are upright when young and hang downward when older. The leaves are undivided, those of the stem narrow and elongate, the basal ones shorter and broader.

Bellflower is a plant of wide distribution and variable size and form. It may occur in open woods—in which case the stems are thin and up to 2 feet in height—but more frequently it is found on gravelly alpine or subalpine ridges where the stems are less than 1 foot in height and are clumped and often somewhat cushion like. The flowers of the alpine form tend to be much larger than those of lowland plants—up to 1 inch in length—fewer in number, and darker in color. Flowering occurs in early summer.

Stems few to several, undivided, 4-24 inches long; leaves of two forms, those of the stems narrow and elongate, basal leaves roundish with long petioles; flowers blue, bell shaped, nodding, 1/2 to 1 inch long; sepals 5, narrow; ovary inferior; fruit a capsule. Campanulaceae.

Mann

Taylor

AMERICAN BISTORT

Polygonum bistortoides
Buckwheat Family

American Bistort is easily recognized by its showy white spikes of densely packed flowers borne on slender stems. The individual flowers are small and not easily discernible within the dense spike. The narrow leaves are rather grass like and mostly basal. As is typical of many members of the Buckwheat family, papery sheaths encircle the stem immediately above each of the few stem leaves.

The widespread and well-known American Bistort is a regular inhabitant of moist mountain meadows throughout the Cascade, Olympic, and Rocky Mountain Ranges. It flowers during early summer.

Stems several, unbranched, slender, 12-24 inches tall; basal leaves elliptical, petioled, 3-6 inches long, with a conspicuous midvein; stem leaves lance shaped, reduced in size; flowers small, with 5 white sepals and no petals, borne in a spike-like inflorescence; fruit an achene. Polygonaceae.

Mann

BOG-ORCHIDS

Habenaria Species — Orchid Family

Bog-orchids are rather tall plants with unbranched succulent stems and strap-shaped, leathery leaves forming sheaths around the stem. The flowers are small and somewhat congested along the upper third of the stem. The floral design is elaborate with 3 upper hooded sepals, a narrow lip-like lower petal, 2 widely spreading lateral petals, and a sac-like spur extending behind the lip.

There are several bog-orchids in the Northwest, found chiefly in wet, boggy sites around lakes and streams and in seepage areas, especially in mountain meadows. Most have unattractive greenish flowers but the beautiful White Bog-orchid (*H. dilatata*) is exceptional with its narrow, spire-like cluster of small creamy-white flowers.

Stems unbranched, succulent, 1-3 feet tall; leaves alternate, strap like, leathery, parallel veined; flowers irregular, spurred, with 6 petals (including sepals); ovary inferior; fruit a capsule with minute seeds. Orchidaceae.

Taylor

UMBRELLA BUCKWHEAT

Eriogonum umbellatum — Buckwheat Family

Umbrella Buckwheat, or Sulphur Flower, is a highly variable species with prostrate woody stems and numerous small rounded leaves that are shiny on the upper side and woolly beneath. The flowers are individually small in dense clusters above a whorl of elongate leaves on an otherwise leafless stalk. Usually the flower clusters are pale (sulphur) yellow but may become reddish with age. In either case, the plants are very attractive with their shiny green foliage and erect balls of flowers.

Umbrella Buckwheat is rather remarkable for its ability to withstand extreme differences in climate, being distributed from the sagebrush deserts to high alpine slopes. It is common throughout the mountain ranges of western North America, occurring on talus slopes or rocky ridges in the Alpine or, less often, the Subalpine Zone. It flowers in late spring.

Matted shrubs, 3-8 inches tall; leaves numerous, 1/2 to 1 inch long, bright shiny green on the upper side, woolly white beneath; flowers small, with 3 sepals and 3 petals, borne in a dense umbel, sulphur yellow to reddish; fruit an achene. Polygonaceae.

Mann

MOUNTAIN BUTTERCUP

Ranunculus eschscholtzii — Buttercup Family

Mountain (or Subalpine) Buttercup is a small, delicate plant, rarely over 8 inches tall, with its leaves deeply dissected into groups of 3 segments. The flowers are about 1/2 inch across with 5 bright-yellow, shiny (waxy) petals. When mature the numerous seeds (achenes) occur in a cone-shaped head. The flowers of buttercups closely resemble those of potentillas or cinquefoils but can be distinguished by their more waxy-shiny petals which have an inconspicuous pocket at their bases. Also, the potentillas are usually hairy plants.

Mountain Buttercup is a frequent inhabitant of moist to wet areas, particularly in rock crevices where there is some water seepage. It occurs in both Alpine and Subalpine Zones and flowers in early summer.

Stems 4-8 inches tall, usually unbranched, succulent, not hairy; leaves dissected into 3-lobed leaflets, mostly basal with long petioles; sepals 5; petals 5, bright shiny yellow, with small basal sacs; stamens numerous; fruits numerous achenes with short, straight beaks, occurring in an elongate cone-shaped head. Ranunculaceae.

Meadow
BUTTERCUP

Mann

WHITE CATCHFLY

Silene parryi — Pink Family

Most species of *Silene* have rather elegant flowers and White Catchfly is no exception. Its petals are white to pale lavender, each having a long, narrow base, 4 terminal lobes, and 2 appendages on the inner face. The sepals are fused into a tube with 5 lobes and 10 greenish to purplish nerves with glandular-sticky hairs. The stems are medium height with 2 to 3 pairs of narrow and elongate, opposite leaves; the other leaves are basal. White Catchfly, which flowers in early summer, is a common member of mountain meadow communities. It is most frequently an associate in sedge and grass communities of the high Subalpine and low Alpine Zones.

Stems several, unbranched, 6-15 inches tall, glandular hairy; leaves opposite and basal, narrow and elongate; sepals glandular, fused with 5 lobes; petals 5, with 4-6 lobes, white to pale lavender, 1/3 inch long; stamens 10; fruit a capsule. Caryophyllaceae.

Taylor

FIELD CHICKWEED

Cerastium arvense — Pink Family

Field Chickweed has showy, white flowers with conspicuously lobed petals. The stems have elongate, opposite leaves and, like the sepals, are usually covered with glandular (sticky) hairs. The fruit is a capsule which opens at the tip, allowing the numerous seeds to be shaken out and scattered by the wind.

This species is equally common in lowland waste areas, along coastal bluffs, and on islands. In the Subalpine and Alpine Zones, it is rarely more than 8 inches in height, often has a cushion appearance, and is found mostly in fine talus or gravelly sites where it flowers during late spring.

Plants low, often matted, usually glandular hairy; leaves opposite, elongate; flowers showy, white; sepals 5; petals 5, deeply lobed, 1/3 to 1/2 inch long; stamens 10; fruit a capsule that splits open at the top. Caryophyllaceae.

Hairy Cinquefoil

Mann

Fanleaf Cinquefoil

Taylor

CINQUEFOIL

Potentilla Species — Rose Family

The bright yellow flowers of cinquefoils closely resemble those of buttercups (*Ranunculus* species) and the two genera are often confused. Buttercups, however, have shinier petals, each with a small basal pouch, and the cinquefoils have small bracts below and alternating with the sepals. The leaves of cinquefoils have 3 or 5 leaflets, the latter situation responsible for the common name meaning "five leaf."

There are several species of *Potentilla* in the Subalpine and Alpine Zones of the Pacific Northwest, among which the Fanleaf Cinquefoil (*P. flabellifolia*) is the most common, being a widespread inhabitant of moist, lush subalpine meadows. It is approximately 1 foot tall with mostly basal, strawberry-like leaves with 3 deeply toothed leaflets. A similar and common species found mostly in alpine meadows, talus slopes, and gravelly ridges is Hairy Cinquefoil (*P. villosa*), a low, compact, cushion-like species with very hairy to woolly leaves. A third common species is Vari-leafed Cinquefoil (*P. diversifolia*) characterized by 5 leaflets rather than 3. It occurs in both the Subalpine and Alpine Zones. The cinquefoils flower in early summer.

Stems several, 1-24 inches tall; leaves compound with 3 or 5 leaflets, usually soft hairy, concentrated near the base of the stem; flowers yellow with 5 sepals (and 5 lower bracts), 5 petals, and numerous stamens; fruits numerous 1-seeded achenes. Rosaceae.

Taylor

SHRUBBY CINQUEFOIL

Potentilla fruticosa — Rose Family

Shrubby Cinquefoil is unique among the potentillas, or cinquefoils, in being woody. It is a low-spreading shrub with numerous attractively divided leaves and many brilliant-yellow, rose-like flowers. Every flower produces several small fruits (achenes), each with an attached tuft of whitish hair. Flowers appear during early summer. This plant forms dense mats on dry, gravelly slopes or rock outcrops in the Alpine or Subalpine Zones. Because of its attractive leaves, showy flowers, and adaptability, it is a desirable garden plant and is widely cultivated.

Low, spreading shrub, 1-2 feet tall; leaves numerous, hairy, divided into 3-7 crowded leaflets; flowers showy, 1 inch wide, numerous; sepals 5, with 5 associated bracts; petals 5, bright yellow; stamens numerous; fruits numerous achenes with tufted hair. Rosaceae.

Mann

COLUMBINE

Aquilegia formosa — Buttercup Family

The red-and-yellow spurred flowers of the Columbine form a handsome, striking contrast to meadow greenery and provide a strong attractant for pollinating bumblebees and hummingbirds, both seeking nectar from a small gland at the base of the spur. The bumblebee chews through the spur and laps up the nectar; the hummingbird hovers near the flower and extracts the nectar by extending its beak into the opening of the spur. The fern-like leaves add to the total attractiveness of the plant.

Columbine occurs in open forests and along forest margins at lower elevations but is most common in moist mountain meadows on gravelly, well-drained sites. It flowers in early summer.

Stems several, branched, 1-3 feet tall; leaves mostly basal, compound in multiples of 3 lobed leaflets; flowers red and yellow, nodding; sepals 5, red; petals 5, with red spurs and yellow blades; stamens numerous; fruits 3-5 follicles with numerous black, shiny seeds. Ranunculaceae.

Cow-parsnip

COW-PARSNIP

Mann

Heracleum lanatum — Parsley Family

Cow-parsnip is a robust herbaceous plant with large palmate leaves and thick, fleshy, hollow stems. The generic name comes from "Hercules," relating to the plant's size; "lanatum" means woolly and refers to the prominent long, woolly hairs, especially on the upper part of the plant. The white flowers are very small with the outer ones of the flat-topped cluster (umbel) being sterile and having showier petals which function only in insect attraction. Cow-parsnip occurs along stream banks and in meadows from the lowlands to moist, subalpine meadows. The roots and peeled stems are edible.

Plants densely hairy, robust, 3-6 feet tall; stems hollow, succulent; leaves up to 1 foot wide, divided into 3 palmately lobed leaflets; petioles expanded at the base sheathing the stem; flowers white, small, in a large, flat-topped umbel with the outer flowers sterile and asymmetrical; fruits flattened and resembling sunflower seeds. Umbelliferae.

Taylor

SLENDER CRAZYWEED

Oxytropis campestris — Pea Family

Slender Crazyweed is recognized by its pea-like, pale yellow flowers and grayish-hairy, pinnately compound leaves. The stems are seldom more than 6 inches tall and, as is typical of members of the pea family, the fruit is a pod (legume).

Slender Crazyweed tends to be restricted to high alpine ridges where it forms occasional dense populations on rocky slopes and in *Carex* (sedge) meadows. It flowers during early summer.

The common name, Crazyweed, is popularly applied to the entire genus *Oxytropis*. In the plains states this genus has toxic properties which cause impaired eyesight and poor muscular co-ordination in livestock. However, Slender Crazyweed probably is not poisonous since mountain goats feed regularly on the plants with no apparent ill effect.

Plants (including sepals) densely hairy; stems several, spreading, 3-6 inches tall; leaves pinnately compound, mostly basal; flowers irregular, pea like, pale yellow, approximately 1/2 inch long; fruit a pod. Leguminosae.

Taylor

MOUNTAIN DAISY

Erigeron compositus
Sunflower Family

Mountain Daisy is one of the most beautiful wild flowers of the high mountains. It has attractive, fern-like basal leaves and showy, solitary heads, each with several pink-to-blue rays surrounding a cluster of yellow disc flowers. Both the stems and leaves are densely and conspicuously hairy.

This is the most common daisy of alpine habitats. It occurs on rocky ridges or fine-talus slopes throughout the high mountains of the Pacific Northwest and Northern Rockies. It flowers in early summer.

Stems few to several, unbranched, 3-6 inches tall; leaves basal (reduced and bract like on the stem), divided at the tips; heads solitary on the stems, 1 inch across; rays pink to blue; disc flowers yellow; pappus of hair-like bristles. Compositae.

Mann

SUBALPINE DAISY

Erigeron peregrinus — Sunflower Family

To many people all daisies look alike. They certainly do tend to be similar and the Subalpine Daisy is rather average in its appearance. The stems are 8 to 24 inches tall; the heads are solitary on unbranched stems; and the numerous rays (approximately 60) are pale blue violet. Some of the mountain asters have similar features but fewer rays.

The Subalpine Daisy ranges from middle elevations—where it occurs in moist forest openings—to meadows of the Subalpine and lower Alpine Zones where it is a late-flowering member of lush meadow communities.

Stems several, unbranched, 8-24 inches tall, shorter and more compact at higher elevations; leaves several inches long, reduced above; heads 2-3 inches across, usually solitary; rays 40-80, blue violet to nearly white; disc flowers yellow; pappus of hair-like bristles. Compositae.

Taylor

DESERT-PARSLEY

Lomatium Species — Parsley Family

There are many species of *Lomatium* in western North America, most occurring in the sagebrush steppe and some extending upward into mountain meadows and onto rocky ridges. Most species have finely divided, fern-like or dill-like basal leaves and one to several upright flowering stems. The numerous yellow or white flowers are borne in an umbrella-like cluster (umbel). Individual flowers are very small with 5 petals, 5 stamens, and no sepals. The roots are usually thick and fleshy and some have been widely collected for food—hence the frequently used common name, Biscuit-root.

The various desert parsleys have similar characteristics and cannot easily be distinguished. The most common montane species of the Cascades and Olympics is the Few-fruited Desert-parsley (*Lomatium martindalei*) which occurs on dry, rocky ridges, especially in the Subalpine Zone. It flowers in the spring.

Stems few to several, usually branched; leaves mostly basal, finely divided and carrot like; flowers small, mostly yellow, borne in umbels; sepals none; petals 5; stamens 5; fruit usually flattened, splitting into 2 halves. Umbelliferae.

Mann

SMOOTH DOUGLASIA

Douglasia laevigata — Primrose Family

Smooth Douglasia is an attractive cushion plant which superficially resembles a number of other mat-formers but is distinguishable by a combination of rose-to-dark-lavender flowers and umbrella-like flower clusters. It is further distinguished from Penstemons of similar color and habit by its trumpet-shaped, regular (radially symmetrical) flowers. The small leaves of Douglasia are rather densely clustered along short branches and at the base of leafless, upright flowering stems.

Douglasia—named in honor of David Douglas, pioneer plant explorer of the Northwest—is an early flowering plant found mostly on very moist talus slopes and ledges in the Alpine or Subalpine Zones of the Western Cascades and Olympics.

Low, mat-forming plants, with numerous small leaves, up to 3/4 inch long; flowers regular, rose to lavender, trumpet shaped with a tubular base and 5 spreading lobes (petals); sepals 5; stamens 5; flowers borne in umbels; fruit a capsule. Primulaceae.

Elephant-head

Taylor   Taylor

ELEPHANT-HEAD

Pedicularis groenlandica — Figwort Family

The quaint reddish-to-purplish flowers which strongly resemble elephant heads make this a strikingly distinctive member of the *Pedicularis* or Lousewort group. The petals are variously fused and modified into a tubular "neck," an up-turned "trunk," and flaring "ears." The slender, purplish stems arise from a number of attractive, fern-like leaves. Elephant-head occurs in both Subalpine and Alpine Zones, in bogs or wherever seepage persists throughout the growing season. It flowers during the summer.

A less common reddish-flowered species is Bird's-beak Lousewort (*P. ornithorhyncha*), with a down-curved, beak-like upper lip. It occurs in moist, gravelly meadows rather than boggy or seepage areas.

Stems few to several, unbranched, 8-16 inches tall; leaves mostly basal, pinnately compound with toothed leaflets; flowers strongly irregular, resembling an elephant's head, reddish to purplish; fruit a capsule. Scrophulariaceae.

Mann

FAIRYBELL

Disporum hookeri — Lily Family

The delicate, creamy-white flowers of Fairybell hang in pairs—like two bells—from the tips of leafy branches. The plants themselves are branched with many bright-green leaves that lack petioles and have conspicuous parallel veins. The fruit is an attractive bright-red berry.

Fairybell is fairly common in the Pacific Northwest where it occurs on rather well-drained slopes of mountain meadows or in open forests at high elevations. A similar but less common species is Fairy-lantern (*D. smithii*) which is more shade tolerant and occurs in montane forests. It is a larger plant with broader and shinier leaves and larger flowers. Both species flower in early summer.

Stems branched and leafy, 12-24 inches tall; leaves ovate, shiny green, with prominent parallel veins, and lacking petioles; flowers creamy white, nodding in pairs, bell shaped, approximately 1/2 inch long; sepals and petals 3, distinguished only by position; stamens 6; ovary superior; fruit a red berry. Liliaceae.

Mann   Mann

GREEN FALSE-HELLEBORE

Veratrum viride — Lily Family

Green False-hellebore is the largest member of the Lily family in the Pacific Northwest, reaching a height of 7 feet. The leaves are also large and have prominent parallel veins. The flowers are green or yellowish green and individually small but densely clustered on long, drooping branches. In particularly moist habitats where the snow melts late, the summer-flowering Green False-hellebore is a co-dominant with Sitka Valerian in lush subalpine meadow communities. The related California False-hellebore (*Veratrum californicum*) is smaller and has white flowers congested in erect spikes. It has a more southern distribution.

The leaves and especially the roots of *Veratrum* are poisonous and have historically been used and misused for medicinal and other purposes. However, the leaves lose their toxicity as they mature, and in some areas, like the northern Rockies, the plants are eaten by elk and called "Elk-weed."

Stems coarse, 3-7 feet tall; leaves 6-12 inches long, 3-6 inches wide, with prominent parallel veins; flowers greenish with parts in multiples of 3; fruit a capsule. Liliaceae.

Mann

FIREWEED

Epilobium angustifolium — Evening Primrose Family

Fireweed is a tall plant with numerous lance-shaped leaves and is well known for its showy rose-to-lavender, 4-petaled flowers borne in a spire-like cluster. The flowers are also a favorite summer nectar source for honeybees, and fireweed honey is widely acclaimed for its excellent flavor.

Fireweed gets its name from its ubiquitous occurrence in burned forest areas where it spreads rapidly by seeds and rhizomes and quickly occupies the entire burned area, providing a brilliant display of color. It is also common in logged sites, along avalanche tracks, and in subalpine meadows. Its wide distribution and consistent occurrence in suitable habitats is due to the light-weight seeds which have a tuft of hair at one end and are readily dispersed by the wind.

Stems 3-6 feet tall, rhizomatous with numerous narrow, lance-shaped leaves; flowers showy in a dense spire-like inflorescence; sepals 4; petals 4, 1 inch long, rose to lavender; stamens 8; ovary inferior; fruit a linear capsule with numerous tufted minute seeds. Onagraceae.

Mann

GLACIER-LILY

Erythronium grandiflorum — Lily Family

The beautiful Glacier-lily is well marked by its bright golden-yellow, nodding flowers with their 6 petals (tepals) reflexed backward and upward. The stems are less than 1 foot tall, bear 1 to 2 showy flowers, and are derived from elongate, edible bulbs. The 2 shiny green leaves with parallel veins are borne at the base of the stem. A white-flowered species, *Erythronium montanum* (Avalanche-lily), is common in the Mt. Rainier area and farther south.

The Glacier-lily is a herald of spring in mountain meadows, where it can frequently be found growing up through melting snow. It sometimes provides an almost continuous coverage over vast meadow areas to be replaced later in the season by the lush growth of numerous other meadow species.

Stems single, 6-12 inches tall, leafless, bearing 1-2 flowers; leaves 2, basal, elliptical, 4-8 inches long, bright green, parallel veined; flowers yellow, nodding, with 6 reflexed tepals; stamens 6; ovary superior; fruit a many-seeded, erect capsule. Liliaceae.

Taylor

NORTHERN GOLDENROD

Solidago multiradiata — Sunflower Family

Northern Goldenrod is a low, loosely matted, leafy plant seldom exceeding 1 foot in height. Several daisy-like heads of showy yellow flowers crown each of many stems. The seeds (achenes) have spreading parachute-like bristles and are widely scattered by the wind—so much a part of the alpine environment.

Northern Goldenrod is a relatively common inhabitant of alpine meadows and fine talus, occurring occasionally in similar but less rigorous habitats of the Subalpine Zone. Flowers appear in early summer.

Plants low, usually matted, 2-18 inches tall; leaves alternate, bright green, slightly toothed, 2-4 inches long (those of the upper stem shorter); heads several per stem, with yellow rays and disc flowers; pappus parachute like, when the seeds are mature. Compositae.

Lyall's Goldenweed

Golden Fleabane

Taylor

Taylor

LYALL'S GOLDENWEED

Haplopappus lyallii — Sunflower Family

Lyall's Goldenweed is a low, glandular-hairy plant with few to several unbranched leafy stems. The showy heads are solitary on the stems and have bright yellow rays and disc flowers.

The summer-flowering Goldenweed grows on gravelly ridges or talus slopes in the Alpine or, less frequently, the Subalpine Zone. A somewhat similar and equally attractive plant is Golden Fleabane (*Erigeron aureus*), a yellow daisy which is found in similar habitats; the ranges of the two species overlap. Golden Fleabane can be distinguished, however, by its essentially non-leafy stems, its long, petioled basal leaves, and its less "ragged" flowering heads with extensive woolly pubescence on the lower side.

Stems 1 to several, unbranched, 2-6 inches tall, leafy, glandular hairy; leaves also glandular, 1/2 to 3 inches long, lance shaped, without petioles; heads 1 inch across with yellow rays and disc flowers; pappus of thread-like bristles. Compositae.

Mann

Mann

FRINGED GRASS-OF-PARNASSUS

Parnassia fimbriata — Saxifrage Family

There is no mistaking the delicate white flowers of the graceful Fringed Grass-of-Parnassus. They arise on rather long, slender stems from glossy, prominently veined, heart- or kidney-shaped leaves. The creamy-white 1/2-inch petals are fringed (fimbriate) with hair-like filaments along the sides of their narrow bases. This characteristic is responsible for the common name.

Fringed Grass-of-Parnassus grows along stream banks, in seepage areas, or bog-like habitats in montane forest openings and subalpine meadows where it flowers in the summertime. The genus derives its name from Mt. Parnassus in Greece.

Stems solitary or few, unbranched, 6-16 inches tall, with a single heart-shaped leaf; basal leaves broadly heart or kidney shaped, prominently veined, on long petioles; flowers solitary, white, with 5 fringed petals and an unusual cluster of sterile stamens opposite each petal; sepals 5; fruit a capsule. Saxifragaceae.

Mann

PINK MOUNTAIN-HEATHER

Phyllodoce empetriformis
Heath Family

There is little that can match the beauty of heather meadows with the delicate bell-shaped flowers and attractive foliage of the dominant pink and white heathers. In the absence of flowers, Pink Mountain-heather can be identified by its numerous needle-like leaves distributed equally along the low, branched stems. The related Yellow Mountain-heather (*Phyllodoce glanduliflora*) closely resembles Pink Heather but has glandular, yellowish-green flowers and occurs at higher elevations.

Pink Mountain-heather is one of the most prominent plants in moist subalpine meadows of the Pacific Northwest. It may also occur, although less frequently, in the upper open forests or in sheltered alpine meadows, particularly where snow melts late. It flowers in early spring or soon after snow melt.

Low, often matted shrubs, 4-16 inches tall; leaves numerous, approximately 1/2 inch long, needle-like, evergreen; flowers pink to red, bell-shaped with 5 lobes, 1/3 inch long, concentrated near the branch tips; sepals 5; stamens 10; fruit a capsule. Ericaceae.

WHITE MOUNTAIN-HEATHER

Cassiope mertensiana — Heath Family

Although the low branches of White Mountain-heather are easily mistaken for club moss (*Selaginella*), the heather is very distinctive when the delicate snow-white, bell-shaped flowers are present. The stems are seldom more than a foot tall and the many branches are covered with small, overlapping, scale-like leaves occurring in 4 rows. A second white-flowered heather of the region is the more restricted and smaller *Cassiope stelleriana* (Moss Heather). White Mountain-heather is a widespread shrub in the Subalpine and lower Alpine Zone. It is usually found in fairly well-drained sites where the snow melts late in spring—which is the time this species flowers.

Low spreading to erect, much-branched shrubs; leaves scale like, overlapping in 4 rows, covering the branches; flowers white, nodding, bell shaped; sepals 5; stamens 10; fruit a capsule. Ericaceae.

Taylor

YELLOW MOUNTAIN-HEATHER

Phyllodoce glanduliflora — Heath Family

Yellow Mountain-heather is a low shrub, never more than a few feet tall, with numerous needle-like leaves. The glandular flowers are greenish yellow, urn shaped, nodding, and are borne at the tips of the branches.

Yellow Mountain-heather is frequently associated with the more showy Pink Mountain-heather, *Phyllodoce empetriformis*, and the two can easily be confused when the distinctive flowers are not available for positive identification. However, Yellow Mountain-heather has glandular hairs on the stems and leaves and is found more frequently on drier sites. It is also much more common in the Alpine Zone where it is sometimes a dominant. It flowers in the summer, later than Pink Mountain-heather.

Low, spreading, glandular-hairy shrubs with numerous needle-like leaves; flowers greenish yellow, urn shaped, or bell like, nodding at branch tips; sepals 5; stamens 10; fruit a capsule. Ericaceae.

Mann

CASCADE HUCKLEBERRY

Vaccinium deliciosum
Heath Family

Cascade Huckleberry is a low, bushy shrub with numerous small fine-toothed leaves and nearly round, pinkish flowers. It is very abundant in the Subalpine and Alpine Zones where it is often associated with one or more of the heathers. It is, however, distributed over a much wider ecological range than heathers, occurring in the upper open forests and around tree clumps—where it grows to heights of 2 feet—and extending upward to dry alpine ridges where it is seldom more than a few inches tall. In the fall the leaves turn bright red or purplish, providing a spectacular display of color around subalpine tree clumps and over vast expanses of meadow area.

As the Latin name suggests, the blue berries are very tasty, particularly when collected from plants grown under a combination of hot afternoons (on south-facing slopes) and sufficient moisture. Flowers are produced in early summer, and fruits during the late summer weeks.

Small extensively branched shrubs, 2-24 inches tall; leaves alternate, 1/2 to 2 inches long, half as wide, fine toothed; flowers round, pinkish, with 5 very short petal lobes; ovary inferior; fruit an edible berry. Ericaceae.

Harsh Paintbrush

Small-flowered Paintbrush

Cliff Paintbrush

Taylor

Taylor

INDIAN-PAINTBRUSH 110 Subalpine-Alpine

Taylor

INDIAN-PAINTBRUSH

Castilleja Species—Figwort Family

The genus *Castilleja* includes a number of strikingly colorful and interesting species of paintbrush, or Indian-paintbrush, which are partially parasitic upon the roots of associated plants such as grasses. The hairy plants have numerous leaves that are usually divided, the upper ones becoming bract like and pigmented. These bracts, together with the sepals, are responsible for the bright coloration of paintbrushes. The inconspicuous petals are greenish and fused together to form a long tube which at maturity extends beyond the colorful sepals.

Among the paintbrushes there are many color variants, from brilliant crimson to yellow or nearly white. The variation in color occurs within species as well as among species, and in the very common Small-flowered Paintbrush (*C. parviflora*), almost every color is represented, the most common being whitish.

The most colorful species in the Pacific Northwest is the brilliant, crimson-colored Cliff Paintbrush (*C. rupicola*) which is relatively common on high alpine, rocky ridges. Harsh Paintbrush (*C. hispida*) is a common lowland species which occasionally reaches mountain meadows. Most species are found in well-drained, sandy or gravelly soil, and with the exception of the common Scarlet Paintbrush (*C. miniata*), they are found only in non-forested areas. Flowering occurs over a long period of time beginning in early summer.

Stems several from a woody root crown, usually densely hairy, 6-18 inches tall; leaves numerous, usually divided, bract like and pigmented above; petals tubular and inconspicuous; sepals 4 lobed and brightly pigmented; fruit a capsule. Scrophulariaceae.

Showy Jacob's-ladder

Elegant Jacob's-ladder

Mann

Taylor

JACOB'S-LADDER

Polemonium Species—Phlox Family

The best identification feature of Jacob's-ladder is the design of its long leaves, which are upright and pinnately compound with numerous pointed leaflets resembling the rungs of a ladder. The stems are generally weak and seldom more than one foot tall. The attractive funnel-shaped flowers are sky blue with yellow centers.

Two common Jacob's-ladders in the Pacific Northwest are *P. pulcherrimum* (Showy Jacob's-ladder) and *P. elegans* (Elegant Jacob's-ladder). The former is taller, more flexuous, and is found from open montane forests to alpine slopes. Elegant Jacob's-ladder is glandular sticky with shorter, more closely compacted leaflets and larger flowers. It occurs in rocky, sheltered alpine habitats. Both species have fern-like leaves and both have an unpleasant skunky odor characteristic of the genus *Polemonium*.

Stems few to several, weak and succulent, 4-12 inches tall; leaves pinnately compound (with sharp-pointed leaflets), mostly basal; flowers funnel shaped with 5 lobes, blue with a yellow center; ovary superior; fruit a capsule. Polemoniaceae.

Plains Larkspur

Pacific Larkspur

Mann

Taylor

PACIFIC LARKSPUR

Delphinium menziesii
Buttercup Family

Larkspurs are exceptional within the Buttercup family in having irregular (bilaterally symmetrical) spurred flowers that are highly adapted to pollination by long-tongued bees which extract nectar from the base of the spur. The flowers have 5 blue-purple sepals, the upper one prolonged into the spur; 4 petals, the upper 2 white with fine blue stripes, the lower 2 blue; and numerous stamens. The leaves, palmately lobed and divided, are borne at or near the base of the stem.

Pacific Larkspur is a frequent and attractive inhabitant of moist but rocky sites in forest openings or meadows from low to high elevations in the mountains. The very common Plains Larkspur (*Delphinium nuttallianum*) occasionally extends upward into montane habitats on the drier, lee side of Pacific Northwest mountains. Both of these species, and others of the region, are poisonous to livestock if consumed in sufficiently large quantities. Pacific Larkspur flowers in late spring.

Stems usually solitary, 8-16 inches tall, often branched; leaves mostly basal, palmately lobed and divided; flowers irregular, borne in an open raceme; sepals 5, blue purple, 1-spurred; petals 4, 2 dissimilar; stamens numerous; fruits 3-5 follicles. Ranunculaceae.

Bracted Lousewort

Taylor

BRACTED LOUSEWORT

Pedicularis bracteosa
Figwort Family

Bracted Lousewort is a tall, unbranched herb with attractive fern-like leaves. The pale-yellowish flowers are interspersed with bracts in a dense spike-like cluster along the stem tip. The flowers are strikingly irregular, the upper petals forming a short hood, the lower ones being shorter and projected outward. This plant is seldom absent from the lush meadows of the Subalpine Zone where it flowers in early summer. The less common Coiled-beak Lousewort (*P. contorta*) is similar but smaller, and the flowers have a pronounced downward-coiled beak.

The common name, Lousewort, comes from *Pedicularis* (Latin for louse) and wort, old English for plant. It reflects the time when plants of this genus were thought to promote lice in livestock.

Stems coarse, few to several, unbranched, 1-3 feet tall; leaves pinnately compound and variously toothed, borne near the base of the stem; flowers pale yellowish, irregular, with an upper hood and 3 lower lobes all borne on a basal tube; sepals 5, glandular hairy; ovary superior; fruit a capsule. Scrophulariaceae.

Taylor

RAMSHORN LOUSEWORT

Pedicularis racemosa—Figwort Family

Like other species of Lousewort (*Pedicularis*), the Ramshorn has strikingly irregular flowers and gets its name from the upper hooked-to-coiled segment of the modified white-to-rose petals. In addition to its unique flowers, the Ramshorn can be distinguished from other species of Lousewort by its finely toothed rather than deeply lobed or pinnate leaves.

The Ramshorn is probably the most common species of Lousewort but not the most attractive. It occurs frequently in moist to rather dry, well-drained sites in upper open forests and subalpine meadows. Only rarely can it be found in the Alpine Zone. It flowers in midsummer.

Stems several, unbranched, leafy, 6-18 inches tall; leaves lance shaped, toothed, 2-4 inches long; flowers irregular with 3 lower petal lobes and an upper "hood" or "horn" about 1/2 inch long; sepals 5; stamens 4; fruit a capsule. Scrophulariaceae.

Meadow   115   **LOUSEWORT**

Broadleaf Lupine

Mann

Taylor

Taylor

LUPINE

Lupinus Species—Pea Family

In addition to being common and attractive, lupines are easily recognized by their irregular, sweet-smelling, pea-like flowers and palmately compound leaves with 6 to 8 spreading leaflets. The plants are usually branched from the base and vary in height according to species. The flowers are blue to purple and white and are borne in dense or elongate, often pyramidal, clusters. The fruits (pods), like the flowers, are typical for the legume family.

Two common species occur in the mountains of the Pacific Northwest, Broadleaf or Subalpine Lupine (*L. latifolius*) and Alpine Lupine (*L. lepidus* var. *lobbii*). The former is a rather tall plant, usually well over 1 foot, and is common throughout the lush meadows of the Subalpine Zone. Alpine Lupine has a low cushion habit with spreading branches. It grows in sandy to gravelly alpine or subalpine habitats. Both species flower during early summer.

Stems few to several, erect or spreading, up to 2 feet tall; leaves palmately compound with 6-8 elongate, hairy leaflets; flowers irregular, pea like; fruit a hairy pod (legume). Leguminosae.

Mann

MARSHMARIGOLD

Caltha biflora—Buttercup Family

Marshmarigold is a succulent plant which is forked at midlength, each of the 2 branches ending with a showy white to pale-yellow flower. The bright, shiny leaves, all basal, are heart or kidney shaped.

Marshmarigold is common along small streams or marshy areas in high meadows. It can be distinguished from various Saxifrages, with which it is often associated, by its numerous stamens and 5 (3 to 6) many-seeded fruits. A closely related species, Elkslip (*Caltha leptosepala*), is frequently found in similar habitats but differs from *C. biflora* in having somewhat elongate leaves and an unbranched stem with a single flower. Both species flower in late spring to early summer.

Stems succulent, 4-14 inches tall, 2-branched; leaves basal, coarsely toothed, broadly heart or kidney shaped, 3-4 inches long, bright shiny green; flowers 2 per plant, approximately 1 inch across; petals none; sepals 7-9, whitish; stamens numerous; fruits 3-6 follicles. Ranunculaceae.

Mann

Taylor

WESTERN
MEADOWRUE

Thalictrum occidentale
Buttercup Family

With its attractive lacy foliage—and when not in flower—Western Meadowrue resembles the closely related Columbine. However, the individual plants of Meadowrue are unisexual. The staminate (male) plants (lower photo) have open clusters of flowers which lack petals but have many colorful yellow or purple stamens which hang like a chandelier from 5 green sepals of each flower. The pistillate (female) flowers (upper photo) have equally reduced flowers, each consisting of 5 sepals and 4 to 10 greenish-purple, spreading ovaries with hairy styles.

Although Western Meadowrue may occur in moist, shady sites, it is most common in lush subalpine meadows, especially avalanche tracks and other well-drained areas. It flowers during early summer.

Plants unisexual, 1-3 feet tall, branched, leafy; leaves divided and lobed into multiples of 3 leaf segments; flowers with 5 green sepals and many stamens or 4-10 ovaries; petals none; fruits achenes. Ranunculaceae.

Pink Monkeyflower

Taylor

Taylor

PINK MONKEYFLOWER

Mimulus lewisii
Figwort Family

The flowers of Pink (or Red) Monkeyflower are particularly showy with their reddish coloration and bilateral symmetry adapted for insect pollination. The petals are fused into a tube with 5 lobes projected outward, 2 upward and 3 downward. The throat of the tube is marked by 2 longitudinal, yellow, hairy ridges which add to the total attractiveness of the flower. One or a few flowers are borne on each branch of the weak, succulent stems with opposite leaves.

Pink Monkeyflower is a frequent inhabitant of small streams and seepage areas of mountain meadows where it provides a brilliant display of color during the summer months.

Stems several, branched, succulent, 1-2 feet tall; leaves opposite, ovate, toothed, prominently veined; flowers pink to red, irregular (2-lipped), with 5 petal lobes, 1-2 inches long; sepals fused into a tube with 5 triangular lobes; ovary superior; fruit a papery, many-seeded capsule. Scrophulariaceae.

Mann

MOUNTAIN MONKEYFLOWER

Mimulus tilingii—Figwort Family

Mountain Monkeyflower is a beautiful plant with densely matted succulent stems and large, showy yellow flowers. The leaves are prominently veined and toothed and are concentrated toward the base of the stem. The flowers are strongly irregular with 2 upper and 3 lower petal lobes projecting from a tubular base with a hairy "throat." The lower lobes (lip) are usually splotched with red, contrasting sharply with the otherwise bright yellow color and providing an attractive landing platform for nectar-seeking, pollinating bees. Mountain Monkeyflower occurs in wet gravelly or sandy sites in the Alpine or Subalpine Zones where it flowers during early summer.

Stems succulent, matted, 2-6 inches tall; leaves mostly basal, roundish, 1/2 to 1 inch long, prominently veined, toothed; flowers irregular, 1 to 1/2 inches long; sepals fused into a tube with 5 triangular lobes; petals fused with 5 unequal lobes, the lower larger and red mottled; fruit a capsule. Scrophulariaceae.

Taylor

MOSS-CAMPION

Silene acaulis—Pink Family

Moss-campion, or Carpet Pink, forms very tightly compressed, round-topped, moss-like mats, never more than an inch or two high but several inches in diameter. Over a period of several years the diameter of each mat increases until eventually the center becomes senescent and dies. Ultimately this leads to disintegration of the mat into several smaller segments, many of which die while others become rejuvenated and repeat the cycle. The tubular pink-to-lavender flowers are produced on very short stalks that arise from the mat of short, needle-like leaves.

Moss-campion is the stereotype cushion plant of the arctic tundra and high, rocky, alpine ridges where the vegetation is subjected to temperature extremes and intense winter-chilling and summer-drying winds.

Mann

The flowers of Moss-campion are produced beginning in early spring and extending over several weeks depending on factors such as exposure and slope. At the time of flowering, Moss-campion is one of the most strikingly colorful plants of the region.

Dense, low, cushion plants, 1-2 inches tall; leaves less than 1/2 inch long, needle like, very numerous; sepals fused, with 5 lobes; petals 5, pinkish; fruit a capsule. Caryophyllaceae.

Meadow   123   **MOSS-CAMPION**

Taylor

MOUNTAIN-AVENS

Dryas octopetala—Rose Family

Mountain-avens is an attractive low shrub which forms dense mats over extensive areas. Its many leaves are evergreen and coarsely toothed with thickened inrolled margins. Its showy white flowers resemble strawberry blossoms but are larger and have more than 5 petals —usually 8 as indicated by the word "octopetala."

Mountain-avens is widely distributed throughout much of the Arctic, extending south along all mountain ranges of western North America. It is a frequent inhabitant of high alpine rocky ridges and peaks in the eastern Cascades. It is an ecologically important species, both as a dominant member of plant communities in which it occurs and as a soil stabilizer on alpine slopes subjected to extreme forces of erosion. Flowers are produced in early summer.

Low, mat-forming shrubs; leaves numerous, 1/2 to 1-1/2 inches long, leathery, evergreen, coarsely toothed; petals 7-8, white, 1/2 inch long; fruits numerous achenes with long, feathery styles when mature. Rosaceae.

Mann

MOUNTAIN-SORREL

Oxyria digyna—Buckwheat Family

Mountain-sorrel is a rather unusual plant with its several stems covered most of their length by small green-to-red flowers borne on weak and often pendent stalks (pedicels). The leaves are roundish to heart or kidney shaped and occur at the base of the plant.

Among the arctic and alpine species of the Northern Hemisphere, Mountain-sorrel is certainly one of the most widely distributed. In the Pacific Northwest it occurs most frequently on alpine talus slopes, glacial moraines, and rock outcrops, usually where relatively moist. It flowers over a long period of time beginning in early summer.

The leaves and stems of Mountain-sorrel have a pleasantly acidic, rhubarb-like flavor, making them a refreshing snack in the mountains.

Stems several, branched, 2-8 inches tall, bearing small flowers most of their length; leaves basal, roundish to heart shaped, acrid and succulent; petals none; sepals 4, green to red; fruit an achene. Polygonaceae.

Meadow 125 **MOUNTAIN-SORREL**

Partridge-foot

Taylor

PARTRIDGE-FOOT
Luetkea pectinata
Rose Family

Partridge-foot spreads by runners and forms extensive carpets of moss-like "bundles" of bright green leaves. The tip of each small leaf is divided in such a manner as to resemble the foot of a partridge. The white petals are rather small and the flowers occur in a spike-like cluster at the tip of an erect 6-inch stem. (The yellow color in the photograph comes from the stamens.) Although Partridge-foot resembles various saxifrages, it can easily be distinguished by its extensively divided leaves and numerous (more than 10) stamens.

Partridge-foot provides a very attractive display of green and white in the mountain regions of the Pacific Northwest. It is an important component of many subalpine and lower alpine communities, especially in well-drained sites. It flowers late in the spring.

Plants mat forming, spreading by runners; leaves concentrated on short branches and at the base of flowering stems, divided at the tip into narrow segments; flowers white, borne in congested racemes; sepals 5; petals 5; stamens numerous; fruit a follicle. Rosaceae.

Taylor

View of North Cascades (Chowder Ridge)
showing autumn coloration of Cascade
Huckleberry (*Vaccinium deliciosum*).

Davidson's Penstemon

Taylor

Taylor

DAVIDSON'S PENSTEMON

Penstemon davidsonii
Figwort Family

Penstemon is a genus noted for its beautiful tubular and irregular flowers. Each flower has 5 stamens (penta-stamens), 4 of which are functional and the other sterile and bearded, resembling a tongue in the throat of the floral tube. From this appearance, a widely used common name for the genus, "beardtongue," is derived.

Davidson's Penstemon is our most attractive beardtongue. It is a cushion plant with numerous small evergreen leaves and many large, showy, purplish flowers. It forms brilliantly colored shrubby mats on rock outcrops and rocky ridges in the Alpine and Subalpine Zones, occasionally extending downward into the continuous forest in similar exposed habitats. The plants flower in late spring.

Low, mat-forming shrubs; leaves numerous, often toothed, evergreen and leathery, 1/2 to 1 inch long; flowers tubular, with 5 petal lobes, irregular, 2-lipped, bright blue-purple to lavender, 1 to 1-1/2 inches long; sepals 5; stamens 5, 4 functional and 1 sterile, the latter bearded; fruit a many-seeded capsule. Scrophulariaceae.

Mann

SMALL-FLOWERED PENSTEMON

Penstemon procerus—Figwort Family

Small-flowered Penstemon has small but attractive dark blue flowers that are tubular and somewhat irregular with 5 petal lobes. Their showiness is enhanced by being congested into crowded whorls along the tips of short stems. The opposite leaves are ovate or lance shaped, non-toothed, and somewhat leathery.

This penstemon is common in subalpine and alpine meadows which become dry in the summer, particularly those of south-facing slopes. Another common species, Cascade Penstemon (*P. serrulatus*), occurs in lower mountain meadows, avalanche tracks, and fine talus areas. It is larger with more stems, toothed leaves, and less densely clustered, larger and showier flowers.

Stems usually solitary, unbranched, 6-12 inches tall, spreading by woody runners or rhizomes; leaves opposite, non-toothed, 1-2 inches long, the lower ovate and petioled, the upper lance shaped and sessile; flowers tubular, irregular, with 5 petal lobes, about 1/2 inch long; sepals 5; stamens 5, 1 sterile; fruit a capsule. Scrophulariaceae.

Meadow**PENSTEMON**

Silky Phacelia

Taylor

Taylor

SILKY PHACELIA

Phacelia sericea
Waterleaf Family

Silky Phacelia is a beautiful plant with its dense spikes of colorful flowers and attractive fern-like leaves covered by soft, silky hair. It is a typical cushion plant with thickly matted leaves and short, erect flowering stems. The flowers are brilliant lavender to purple or blue with the stamens projected well beyond the fused petals, giving the flower cluster a fuzzy appearance. It is an alpine species, found along gravelly ridges and on talus slopes, often below snow fields. It flowers over a period of several weeks beginning in the early alpine springtime.

Low cushion plants, 4-8 inches tall; leaves numerous, matted, deeply and irregularly cleft, silky white; flowers showy, congested into a spike-like inflorescence; sepals 5; petals 5, bluish, fused at the base; stamens 5, extended beyond the petals; fruit a capsule. Hydrophyllaceae.

WHITELEAF
PHACELIA

Phacelia hastata
Waterleaf Family

The variable Whiteleaf Phacelia may be low and somewhat cushion like (alpine forms) or up to 2 feet tall. The white-hairy leaves are long and rather narrow, frequently having a pair of small ear-like lobes near the base of the blades. The flowers are generally white, although shades of lavender may be encountered, and they are densely grouped in coiled clusters (inflorescences). The stamens extending beyond the fused petals and the densely hairy sepals give the inflorescence a bristly appearance. Whiteleaf Phacelia occurs on dry, gravelly slopes from the foothills of the eastern slopes of the Cascades into the Subalpine and Alpine Zones and flowers during summer months.

Plants densely hairy, 4-24 inches tall; leaves silky hairy, elongate, sometimes lobed at the base; flowers 1/3 inch long, borne in several coiled clusters; sepals 5, hairy; petals 5, fused at the base, white to lavender; stamens 5; fruit a capsule. Hydrophyllaceae.

Taylor

SPREADING PHLOX

Phlox diffusa—Phlox Family

The name "Phlox" is derived from the Greek word for flame and refers to the showy, often brightly colored flowers which have long tubular bases and perpendicularly spreading petal lobes. The flowers are borne singly on short, erect branches covered with narrow, rigid leaves. However, because the branches are so numerous, the plants exhibit a low, almost continuous mass of color which varies from white to pinkish or pale blue. The color variation is an expression of genetic differences and age of the flowers.

Large mats of spreading Phlox can be found on most dry, rocky slopes or rock outcrops in the Pacific Northwest, from the upper Continuous Forest Zone to the Alpine Zone where it flowers in rather early spring. There are other species of Phlox in the Pacific Northwest but none as widespread or common as *Phlox diffusa*.

Low cushion plant with prostrate woody stems; leaves opposite, narrow, rigid and sharp pointed, 1/4 to 3/4 inch long, congested on short stems; flowers pink or blue to white, trumpet shaped, 3/4 inch across; sepals 5, fused; petals 5, fused; stamens 5; fruit a capsule. Polemoniaceae.

Rosy Pussy-toes

Taylor

Taylor

PUSSY-TOES

Antennaria Species
Sunflower Family

Pussy-toes, or Everlastings, represent the Pacific Northwest version of the edelweiss of the Austrian Alps. They are white-woolly plants that spread by runners or rootstalks and often form extensive leafy mats. The upright stems from these mats vary in height from 6 to 12 inches in *Antennaria lanata* to 1 to 4 inches in *A. alpina*. The minute flowers occur in small heads which are clustered into an asymmetrical ball or imaginary cat's paw, each head being a toe. Although the heads have no rays, the outer (involucral) bracts are white to brownish or sometimes pink.

Two common Pussy-toes of the Northwest are Woolly Pussy-toes (*A. lanata*) and Rosy Pussy-toes (*A. rosea*), the latter often having attractive rose-colored bracts. These and other species are well represented along rather dry and rocky montane ridges and in equivalent habitats in the Alpine Zone. Flowering occurs over several summer weeks.

Low, mat-forming, woolly plants with short, erect flowering stems; leaves mostly basal, densely woolly white, 1 to few inches long; heads several, densely clustered with white or colored bracts; rays none; disc flowers minute, yellowish. Compositae.

Taylor

LYALL'S ROCKCRESS

Arabis lyallii—Mustard Family

Lyall's Rockcress is one of the showiest of several species of *Arabis* inhabiting the mountains of the Pacific Northwest. It has several un-branched stems arising from a cushion-like base of many leaves. The urn-shaped flowers are light to dark reddish-purple with 4 unfused petals and 4 sepals. The fruits are flattened, elongate, and erect or spreading. At maturity the fruits split open, the two halves separating from a papery central partition on which the winged seeds are borne. This fruit type is typical of the mustard family.

Arabis lyallii, *A. lemmonii*, and a third species, *A. microphylla*, are frequent inhabitants of rocky ridges or talus slopes in the Alpine or Subalpine Zones. All have similarly colored flowers, cushion habits, and ecological requirements, and they are difficult to distinguish. They flower in the spring and early summer.

Stems several, unbranched, 4-12 inches tall; leaves narrow, approximately 1 inch long, mostly basal; flowers regular, urn shaped, reddish purple, up to 1/2 inch long; sepals 4; petals 4; stamens 6; fruit 1-3 inches long, flattened, capsule like. Cruciferae.

Taylor

ROSEROOT

Sedum rosea—Stonecrop Family

Typical of *Sedum* (Stonecrop) species, Roseroot is a low, succulent plant that spreads by rootstalks. The rubbery, strongly flattened leaves are crowded and appear stacked along the short stems. The flowers are congested into a dense terminal cluster; and the fleshy petals have the unusual color of purplish red, unique among the Northwest species of Sedum.

Roseroot is not common in the Pacific Northwest nor is it particularly showy. It is, however, a widely distributed plant and can occasionally be found growing in fine gravelly soils of high alpine ridges where it flowers in early summer.

Stems unbranched, very succulent, 2-8 inches tall; leaves numerous, flat and rubbery, approximately 1/2 inch long; flowers small, reddish purple, congested at the stem tip; sepals 5; petals 5, fleshy; stamens 10; fruit a capsule; plants unisexual. Crassulaceae.

Meadow
135
ROSEROOT

Dotted Saxifrage

Spotted Saxifrage

Taylor

Alpine Saxifrage   Mann

Taylor   **SAXIFRAGES**

Saxifraga Species
Saxifrage Family

The saxifrages are attractive plants with many rather delicate whitish flowers. The leaves are mostly basal, usually glossy, and often toothed. In the Pacific Northwest there are several species, most of them found in moist to wet habitats in the Subalpine or Alpine Zones. They generally flower in early summer.

Mann

Spotted Saxifrage (*S. bronchialis*) is an attractive cushion plant with relatively large white petals, each with several orange to dark-red spots. The leaves are small, needle-like, and numerous. It is most frequently found on dry, rocky slopes and in rock crevices in the Subalpine and Alpine Zones. The name *"Saxifraga,"* which means "rock breaker," truly applies to this plant.

Alpine Saxifrage (*S. tolmiei*) is another common mat-forming species of the Subalpine and Alpine Zones. It occurs in gravelly sites—such as talus and glacial moraines—that remain moist throughout most of the growing season. It is easily distinguished by its small (1/4 to 1/2 inch long), succulent, club-shaped basal leaves. The flowering stems are short, 2 to 4 inches tall, and bear only one or few flowers. Western Saxifrage (*S. occidentalis*) is another alpine and subalpine species. It has oblong, toothed, leathery and somewhat evergreen leaves.

Dotted Saxifrage (*S. punctata*) is very abundant along streams from the upper forests to the Subalpine Zone. It can be distinguished by its round, heart-shaped to kidney-shaped leaves with scalloped margins, borne on long, weak petioles. A similar saxifrage also found along streams is Brook Saxifrage (*S. arguta*) which has roundish, rather than elongate, petals and more sharply toothed leaves.

Stems mostly leafless and unbranched below the inflorescence; 2-16 inches tall; leaves all basal, variable in size and shape; flowers white, small, with 5 sepals, 5 petals, and 10 stamens; fruit a "twin capsule." Saxifragaceae.

Meadow **SAXIFRAGE**

Mann

ARROWHEAD
SENECIO

Senecio triangularis
Sunflower Family

Although Arrowhead Senecio is one of the many daisy-like species in the often difficult sunflower family, it can readily be identified by its characteristic arrowhead-shaped leaf blades. The stems are 1 to 5 feet tall and leafy throughout. The numerous yellow heads are arranged in a flat-topped cluster.

Arrowhead Senecio is abundant in the mountains of the Pacific Northwest, and dense populations provide splashes of golden-yellow color to lush subalpine meadows where it flowers in the summer.

Stems several, unbranched below the inflorescence, 1-5 feet tall, leafy throughout; leaf blades arrowhead shaped, 2-8 inches long; lower leaves with long petioles; heads several in a flat-topped cluster, with yellow rays and disc flowers; pappus of thread-like bristles. Compositae.

Taylor

SHOOTING-STAR

Dodecatheon Species
Primrose Family

Shooting-stars, widely recognized for their unique floral structure and bright colors, have been given a variety of regional common names including Cowslip and Rooster-head. The name *Dodecatheon* is Greek, meaning 12 gods. Presumably, the attractive plants were protected by these gods.

The showy flowers are reddish to pale lilac and are borne on leafless stems. The 5 petals are reflexed backward from the colorful stamens and extended style, giving the impression of rapid forward movement of a streamlined, star-shaped object.

Few-flowered Shooting-star (*Dodecatheon pauciflorum*) is the most widespread species in the Pacific Northwest, ranging from grasslands to mountain meadows, where it favors seepage areas or habitats kept moist by melting snow. It flowers very early in the spring.

Stems unbranched, 4-10 inches tall, with a terminal umbel of few to several flowers; leaves all basal, narrowly elliptical, rather leathery; flowers showy, reddish to lilac; sepals 5; petals 5, reflexed; stamens 5, enlarged and compressed; fruit a capsule. Primulaceae.

Taylor

ALPINE SMELOWSKIA

Smelowskia calycina—Mustard Family

Alpine Smelowskia is a low cushion plant with many basal, pinnately divided leaves which are grayish in color from numerous microscopic, star-shaped hairs. The flowers are rather densely clustered at the stem tips and have 4 white petals. A closely related plant, *Smelowskia ovalis*, has a similar distribution.

Among the coarse rocks and rock crevices of alpine ridges and peaks, the Smelowskias are widely distributed in the Pacific Northwest. Although not as attractive as most alpine flowering plants, they must be respected for their ability to grow and reproduce in the non-hospitable high alpine "rock piles" where they flower in late spring.

Low cushion plants with numerous grayish-hairy, pinnately compound leaves; flowers in dense racemes at the tip of upright stems; sepals 4; petals 4, white; stamens 6; fruit capsule-like. Cruciferae.

Taylor   Mann

CUSICK'S SPEEDWELL

Veronica cusickii
Figwort Family

There are two common speedwells in the mountainous regions of the Pacific Northwest, Cusick's Speedwell and Alpine Speedwell (*V. wormskjoldii*). Both are small, delicate plants with dark blue, slightly irregular (bilaterally symmetrical) flowers which have the unusual combination of 4 petals and 2 stamens. The two species can be distinguished by their flowers; those of Cusick's Speedwell are larger and showier with the stamens and styles conspicuously extended beyond the petals.

Both are inhabitants of moist meadows of the Subalpine Zone and occasionally extend upward into lower alpine habitats where they are often associates of heather communities. They flower in rather early spring.

Stems single, unbranched, 2-6 inches tall; leaves opposite, oval to oblong, up to 1 inch long; flowers borne in a congested raceme; sepals 4; petals 4, dark blue, less than 1/2 inch wide; ovary superior; fruit a heart-shaped capsule. Scrophulariaceae.

Taylor

WESTERN SPRINGBEAUTY

Claytonia lanceolata
Purslane Family

Western Springbeauty is a widespread and well-known plant, marked by its white to pink flowers with darker pink or red stripes (a yellow-flowered form occurs in the North Cascades). The succulent stems are weak and contorted; and 1 to several are derived from a deeply buried starchy bulb that is edible when cooked. Each stem has a pair of lance-shaped leaves borne immediately below the elongate flower cluster (inflorescence).

Springbeauty and Glacier-lily (*Erythronium grandiflorum*) are usually the first plants to flower in the subalpine meadows, both often extending through the trailing edge of receding snow fields. Both also occur in the Alpine Zone, usually in well-drained areas.

Stems few to several, contorted, 3-8 inches tall, derived from bulbs; leaves 2, opposite, lance-shaped, 1/2 to 3 inches long (1-2 basal leaves sometimes present); flowers several, in 1-sided racemes; sepals 2; petals 5, white to pink, striped; stamens 5; fruit a capsule. Portulacaceae.

Taylor

STONECROP

Sedum Species—Stonecrop Family

The several yellow-flowered species of *Sedum* have a characteristic succulent form and brilliant star-shaped flowers congested in terminal clusters. They are difficult to distinguish from each other, however, and there has been no attempt to do so here. The most common alpine species in the Pacific Northwest is probably *Sedum lanceolatum* (Lanceleaved Stonecrop) which has roundish, narrow, lance-shaped leaves that overlap along the stem and occur in basal clusters as well. The plants spread by rootstalks (rhizomes) and often form loose mats.

Stonecrops occur on rock outcrops and dry, gravelly ridges at essentially all altitudes up to and including the Alpine Zone. They flower in late spring.

Plants very succulent, 2-8 inches tall, with erect flowering stems and densely leafy short shoots, spreading by rhizomes and often forming mats; leaves short, thick, and often pointed; flowers bright yellow, star shaped with 5 pointed petals; sepals 5; fruits 5 follicles per flower. Crassulaceae.

Taylor

EDIBLE THISTLE

Cirsium edule—Sunflower Family

Thistles are stereotyped by most people as noxious weeds and indeed most of them are. However, the Edible Thistle is both attractive and non-weedy, despite having typical spiny leaves and stems. It is a tall plant with thick, succulent stems and large, showy, red-to-purple heads. The entire plant—especially the heads—is covered with long, cobwebby hairs.

Edible Thistle is an occasional member of lush subalpine meadow communities where it flowers in midsummer. The name *edule* refers to the edibility of the starchy or sugary taproot and tender, peeled stem.

Robust herbs, 2-4 feet tall and 1-3 inches thick; leaves several, variously lobed and spiny, several inches long; heads 2-3 inches wide, surrounded by spiny bracts with cobwebby hairs; rays none; disc flowers very numerous, pale red to purple; pappus parachute like. Compositae.

Taylor

TIGER-LILY

Lilium columbianum
Lily Family

The Tiger-lily is one of the most beautiful and best known wild flowers of the Pacific Northwest. It is a tall, graceful plant which usually stands above associated vegetation, sprinkling the meadows and roadsides where it occurs with bright orange color. The leaves are rather large and attractive in one or more whorls near midlength of the stem. The flowers nod and the showy orange petals—with conspicuous red to purple spots—are bent backward and thus upward.

The Tiger-lily has a wide elevational range in the Pacific Northwest, occurring from sea level well upward into the Subalpine Zone where it is common in moist, lush meadows. It flowers in early summer.

Stems single, unbranched, 2-4 feet tall, with bulbs; leaves lance shaped, in 1-2 whorls near midlength of the stem; flowers showy, nodding, with 6 orange, red-spotted, reflexed petals; fruit a capsule with tightly stacked, flat, winged seeds. Liliaceae.

Bee on Flower Cluster

Mann

Mann

SITKA VALERIAN

Valeriana sitchensis—Valerian Family

The tall Sitka Valerian stands like a sentinel above most associated species. It has conspicuous rounded or flat-topped clusters of small, fragrant white flowers that attract bees and butterflies and add to the total beauty of the meadow habitat. Its leaves are large and pinnately compound, the terminal leaflets being larger than the others. The entire plant is succulent and when crushed or broken gives off an unpleasant medicinal odor.

Sitka Valerian is frequently a summer dominant of subalpine meadows that are marked with Springbeauties and Glacier-lilies early in spring. It occurs most abundantly in moist but well-drained soils.

Stems branched, rather succulent, 2-4 feet tall; leaves long petioled, pinnately compound, the terminal leaflet the largest, leaflets toothed; flowers white, slightly irregular, 5-lobed with the stamens and style extended beyond the lobes; ovary inferior; fruit an achene with an umbrella-like protuberance. Valerianaceae.

Taylor

FENDLER'S WATERLEAF

Hydrophyllum fendleri—Waterleaf Family

The outstanding characteristic of Fendler's Waterleaf is the nature of its rather large, somewhat fleshy, fern-like leaves. Its attractive funnel-shaped flowers are white or reddish and occur in rather dense, coiled clusters at the tips of the succulent, leafy stems. The dark-colored stamens (anthers) extend well beyond the petals and contribute to the general showiness of the flowers.

Fendler's Waterleaf is a common component of moist, mountain meadow communities, especially in avalanche tracks in the Subalpine Zone. It also occurs in forest openings at mid-elevations and is replaced on the lowlands by the very similar shade-tolerant Pacific Waterleaf (*H. tenuipes*). Both of these waterleafs flower in late spring or early summer.

Stems succulent, weak, spreading, leafy, 1-2 feet tall; leaves up to 1 foot long, pinnately compound with toothed and lobed leaflets; flowers 1/3 to 1/2 inch long, white to reddish or purple, congested into a coiled inflorescence; sepals 5; petals (lobes) 5; stamens 5, dark, extended beyond the petal lobes; fruit a capsule. Hydrophyllaceae.

Taylor

PAYSON'S WHITLOW-GRASS

Draba paysonii—Mustard Family

There are several species of *Draba* occurring in the high mountains in the Pacific Northwest, most being low cushion plants with yellow or white flowers. Payson's Whitlow-grass is one of the most attractive and certainly the most common of the several species. It has bright yellow flowers with 4 petals and 4 sepals. The minute and hairy leaves are densely matted at the base of the short, flowering stalks. The fruits are ovate and also hairy.

Payson's Whitlow-grass is a frequent inhabitant of high alpine rock outcroppings and crevices, often so barren and devoid of soil that little but lichens successfully grow there. It blooms so early in the season that the flowers are seldom seen except at very high, sheltered sites.

Low, densely matted cushion plants, the stems leafless and rarely more than 2 inches tall; leaves very numerous, all basal, minute, less than 1/2 inch long and a fraction as wide; flowers bright yellow, small, borne in racemes; sepals 4; petals 4; stamens 6; fruit an ovate "capsule." Cruciferae.

Taylor

ALPINE
WILLOW-HERB

Epilobium alpinum
Evening Primrose Family

Alpine Willow-herb is highly variable in size and form. The plants usually have several more or less upright stems, from 2 to several inches tall. The leaves are opposite—or sometimes alternate near the stem tip —and ovate to elliptical. The 4 small petals are 1/4 to 1/3 inch long, notched at the tip, and variable in color from white to dark rose. The linear capsules split at maturity releasing numerous seeds, each with a tuft of long hair at one end, thus aiding in wind dissemination.

Alpine Willow-herb ranges from the arctic into high mountain regions of western North America. It occurs most frequently in rather lush mountain meadows but is common in and around seepage areas and can be found on wet, gravelly alpine slopes. It flowers in early summer.

Stems several, unbranched, 2-12 inches tall; leaves mostly opposite, ovate or narrower, up to 2 inches long; flowers less than 1/2 inch long; sepals 4; petals 4, white-rose, notched at the tip; stamens 8; ovary inferior; capsule elongate and linear. Onagraceae.

Taylor

RED WILLOW-HERB

Epilobium latifolium—Evening Primrose Family

Red Willow-herb is similar to Fireweed (*Epilobium angustifolium*) but is considerably shorter with smaller and fewer leaves. Like those of the Fireweed, the flowers are large and showy but do not occur in dense, spire-like clusters (inflorescences). The 4 attractive, rose to reddish-purple petals are about 1 inch long and rounded at the tip. The 4 lance-shaped sepals are conspicuous between the petals and contribute to the beauty of the radially symmetrical flowers. The ovary develops into a narrow elongate capsule which produces numerous woolly-tufted seeds that blow in the wind, thus maintaining a wide range for the species.

Red Willow-herb is most often found on fine-talus slopes of alpine or subalpine ridges. Occasionally it occurs along the sandy or gravelly banks of mountain streams. It flowers during early summer.

Stems several, unbranched, spreading and erect, 8-14 inches tall; leaves numerous, opposite, lance shaped, 1-2 inches long; sepals lance shaped, 4; petals rounded, 4, reddish to purplish; stamens 8; ovary inferior; fruit a linear capsule with numerous tufted seeds. Onagraceae.

Taylor

YELLOW
WILLOW-HERB

Epilobium luteum
Evening Primrose Family

Yellow Willow-herb is different from other species of *Epilobium* in having yellow flowers. As in other species, however, the flower parts are in multiples of 4 and the ovary matures into a long capsule with numerous tufted seeds. The stems are approximately 1 foot tall and have several ovate to lance-shaped leaves. The pale yellow petals are approximately 1/2 inch long and notched at the tip. This plant is an occasional inhabitant of somewhat boggy or seepage sites in subalpine meadows or montane forest openings and is usually associated with various species of Saxifrage. It flowers in late spring.

Stems leafy, unbranched, rhizomatous, 6-16 inches tall; leaves opposite, ovate, toothed, 1-3 inches long; flowers few to several, borne at the stem tip; sepals 4, lance shaped; petals 4, yellow, heart shaped, 1/2 inch long; stamens 8; ovary inferior; fruit a linear capsule with numerous tufted seeds. Onagraceae.

Taylor

YARROW

Achillea millefolium
Sunflower Family

Yarrow is a well-known plant easily recognized by its flat-topped cluster of small white (or pinkish) heads, its finely divided fern-like leaves, and the strong sage-like odor given off by its leaves when crushed. At low elevations Yarrow may be more than 2 feet tall but in the high mountains it is much smaller, often forming dense populations. It was named for the Greek Achilles, presumably because he used it to treat the wounds of soldiers. In recent years the leaves have been used extensively as a base for a fragrant and "minty" tart tea.

Yarrow is found in many habitat types from desert to moist temperate to high alpine. It is not shade tolerant, however, so cannot grow successfully in forested areas. In the Pacific Northwest, Yarrow is common in rocky, alpine, or occasionally subalpine habitats from near timberline to over 7,500-foot elevations. It flowers in midsummer.

Stems mostly solitary and unbranched, from a few inches to 2-1/2 feet tall, rhizomatous; leaves very finely divided, aromatic; flowers very small in flat-topped clusters of many heads; rays 3-5, white to pink; disc flowers yellow; pappus none. Compositae.

IDENTIFICATION KEY

There is a tendency for the untrained botanist to shy away from identification keys because of a preconceived notion that they are non-functionally complicated, both in construction and language. With familiarity, however, apprehension is replaced by confidence and "walking" through a key can be like a treasure hunt. In this key, usage of floral and foliar terms can be resolved with reference to the illustrations on pages 10 to 13, in the Introduction, and to the Glossary.

The following is a dichotomous two-branched key. At every numerical point the user must decide between two choices (a or b). After having made his or her choice, the user will be provided with a name or will be directed to proceed to another point, as indicated, in the key until a name is eventually derived. The descriptive alternatives should be read carefully and completely before a choice is made.

1a. Tall shrubs, 2-1/2 feet or more in height, usually in or bordering forested areas, or occasionally in lower mountain meadows............................... 2

1b. Smaller shrubs *or* herbs, of various habitats including forests and meadows........................... 15

2a. Flowers approximately 1 inch across *and* stamens *more* than 10; fruit raspberry-like 3

2b. Flowers smaller *or* with 10 or fewer stamens; fruit not raspberry-like 4

3a. Flowers pink to red; leaves divided into 3 leaflets ...
.... *Rubus spectabilis* page 53

3b. Flowers white; leaves broad and lobed (maple-like) but not divided into distinct leaflets *Rubus parviflorus* page 62

4a. Stems and sometimes leaves spiny 5

4b. Stems and leaves without spines or prickles 6

5a. Leaves large, more than 8 inches wide.............
.... *Oplopanax horridum* page 26

5b. Leaves less than 3 inches wide .... *Ribes lacustre* page 25

6a. Leaves pinnately compound, leaflets toothed 7

6b. Leaves simple, *not* pinnately compound (See *Osmaronia* page 39) 9

16a. Aquatic plants with roundish floating leaves and large yellow flowers...........*Nuphar polysepalum* page 46

16b. Plants not as described above 17

17a. Flowers densely clustered into a spike (spadix) with an associated yellow modified leaf (spathe); leaves large, as much as 3 feet long and half as wide at maturity ....*Lysichitum americanum* page 55

17b. Flowers not associated with a yellow spathe; leaves very much smaller............................. 18

18a. Plants either white or reddish, *without green leaves or stems* (non-photosynthetic) 19

18b. Plants bearing green leaves (photosynthetic) 21

19a. Plants white throughout; flower solitary and nodding.......................*Monotropa uniflora* page 38

19b. Plants reddish at least in part; flowers more than one 20

20a. Flowers irregular (bilaterally symmetrical) and orchid-like ....*Corallorhiza* species page 22

20b. Flowers regular (radially symmetrical) and not orchid-like. *Hypopitys monotropa* (and related Ericads) page 44

21a. Flowers bright yellow or orange, not reddish 22

21b. Flowers other than bright yellow or orange......... 25

22a. Plants sunflower-like with large yellow heads; leaves heart-shaped, several inches long and half as wide ...
........................*Balsamorhiza sagittata* page 17

22b. Plants not sunflower-like; leaves smaller *or* pinnately compound 23

23a. Flowers orange; leaves clustered (3 or more) near mid-length of the stem ....*Lilium columbianum* page 145

23b. Flowers yellow; leaves not clustered near mid-length of the stem 24

24a. Leaves pinnately compound with spines along the margins of the leaflets; flowers borne in 1 or more terminal, elongate clusters ....*Berberis nervosa* page 41

24b. Leaves simple, heart-shaped; flowers pansy-like and not clustered.....................*Viola* species page 71

163

GLOSSARY

Achene—A small, dry and hard 1-seeded fruit which functions directly as a single seed.

Alternate—In reference to leaves, one per node, not opposite, borne singly along the stem.

Basal—In reference to leaves, borne at the base of the stem, on the rootcrown.

Biennial—A plant that lives two years, the first year it produces a rosette of leaves, the second a flowering stem.

Bilaterally symmetrical—In reference to floral structure, one or more of the petals (or sepals) are different from the other petals (or sepals); the flower has two similar sides (left and right); it can be dissected only in a vertical plane to produce mirror images (see radially symmetrical).

Blade—The flat part of a leaf or petal.

Bract—A small modified leaf, usually at the base of a flower or flower cluster.

Bulb—A thickened, underground storage or reproductive organ.

Capsule—A fruit which becomes dry and splits open at maturity to shed its seeds.

Compound—In reference to a leaf, a compound leaf is one which is divided to the midvein thus producing 2-many leaflets or leaf segments.

Congested—Crowded.

Conifer—A cone-bearing tree or shrub, a gymnosperm, for example, Douglas Fir.

Coniferous—Adjectival form of conifer.

Cushion—Low and dense structure, like the cushion of a chair.

Dehiscent—In reference to fruits, splitting open at maturity to shed the seeds, for example, a pod.

Disc flower—One of the several radially symmetrical flowers of the Composite family, the central flowers.

Dominant—A species which has a major effect on associated vegetation, one of the most important members of a plant community.

Elliptical—A squashed circle, an ellipse, narrowly oval, not egg-shaped.

Elongate—Lengthened, usually long and narrow.

Evergreen—Relating to leaves, persistent through the winter therefore of coarse texture, leathery and usually shiny.

Flexuous—Narrow and easily bent (as in the wind), limber.

Follicle—One of two or more dehiscent fruits of a single flower, capsule-like.

Fruit—The reproductive organ containing the seeds, for example a capsule, a berry, etc.; derived from the ovary and (sometimes) associated tissues.

Glandular—Having glands or hairs which produce a sticky, resinous material.

Head—A dense cluster of sessile (non-stalked) flowers, for example in compositae (sunflower family).

Herb—A plant lacking hard or tough woody tissue above ground.

Hooded—Having a hood; in reference to a flower, some part(s) arced over the flower in the manner of a hood.

Inferior—In reference to an ovary, the ovary borne below the other flower parts, the flower parts borne on the ovary.

Inflorescence—A flower cluster.

Irregular—In reference to a flower, bilaterally symmetrical or asymmetrical.

Krummholz—Relates to an area of dwarf or shrubby tree growth at and above the timberline.

Leaflet—One of the leaf-like segments of a compound leaf.
Linear—Long and very narrow, with parallel margins, like a line.
Lobed—Divided or cut part way to the center.

Montane—Of the mountains; as used here, denoting that area of the mountains below the timberline, below the alpine and above the lowlands.

Nodding—Relating to flowers, hanging downward, the throat of the flower facing downward.

Oblong—Longer than broad.
Opposite—In relating to leaves, two per node; borne in pairs along the stem.
Oval—Broadly elliptical.
Ovary—The female reproductive structure, seed-bearing part of the flower.
Ovate—Egg-shaped.

Palmate—Parts (for example, leaflets or lobes) radiating outward like the fingers of a hand.
Pappus—Hair-like material produced on the achenes of some composites.
Pedicel—The stalk of a flower or fruit.
Pendent—Hanging down.
Petal—An inner bract-like structure of the flower, usually brightly colored or white.
Petiole—A leaf stalk.
Petiolate—Having a leaf stalk.
Petioled—Having a leaf stalk.
Pinnate—In reference to leaves, leaflets, lobes etc., arranged on each side of a central axis; feather-like.

Raceme—An elongate, unbranched flower cluster, each flower on a short or long stalk or pedicel.
Radially symmetrical—In reference to a flower, all parts of the petals (and sepals) alike; the flower can be dissected along more than one plane to produce mirror images.
Ray—The strap-like or petal-like blade of a ray flower of the composite (sunflower) family.
Ray flower—One of the outer flowers of some composites that has a flattened, petal-like blade or ray.
Reflexed—Bent abruptly backward.
Regular—In reference to a flower, radially symmetrical.
Rhizomatous—Having rhizomes.
Rhizome—An underground rotting stem that produces upright, leafy stems from its nodes; it aids in non-sexual reproduction and horizontal spreading of plants.
Rootstalk—A rhizome.
Rootcrown—The top of the root from which one or more stems or leaves are derived.
Runner—A horizontal stem that grows along the ground sending stems up and roots down.

Sepal—One of the outer bract-like components of a flower, usually green.
Sessile—Non-stalked, in reference to leaves (non-petiolate) or flowers (non-pedicellate).
Shrub—A low woody plant which branches at or near the ground.
Spike—An elongate cluster of sessile or non-stalked flowers.
Spur—Hollow sac-like (usually nectar containing) extension of a sepal or petal.
Stamen—The pollen-bearing organ of the flower.

171

Style—The extension of the ovary, connecting the ovary with the pollen receptive stigma.

Superior—In reference to an ovary, the ovary borne above the point of derivation of the other floral parts.

Succulent—Soft and juicy; fleshy.

Talus—Loose gravel or boulders, usually on a slope.

Tepal—A term used for a petal or sepal when these are similar in size and color (distinguishable only by position).

Umbel—An umbrella-like flower cluster, the flower stalks all derived from the same point at the stem tip.

Understory—The vegetation of the forest floor including shrubs.

Unisexual—One sex, either male (staminate) or female (pistillate).

Urn-shape—Shaped like an urn, big at the bottom and the top and slender in the middle.

Vein—The nerve-like line or lines along leaves and other plant organs.

Whorl—In reference to leaves or flowers, a group of 3 or more borne at a single point or node.

INDEX OF LATIN NAMES

173

INDEX OF COMMON NAMES

175